Seek

Two Companies

EBED
PUBLICATIONS
In love, serve one another

by

Cynthia Duggan

EBED Publications is a division of McDougal
Publishing, Hagerstown, Maryland.

Published by:

EBED Publications
P.O. Box 3595
Hagerstown, MD 21742-3595

ISBN 1-884369-58-8

Printed in the United States of America
For Worldwide Distribution

DEDICATION

To my parents, REVS. CHARLES AND JAN GROOMS:

DAD, because of your prayer for life and your commitment and dedication to be a "seeker," I was born. You showed me first-hand the example of a loving father and made it easy for me to see and understand the nature of my heavenly Father.

MOM, you have been a loving parent, faithful friend, and teacher. You have taught me so many things that have carried me and brought me through life's challenges. Your pursuit of excellence in ministry, love in the face of adversity, and unwavering commitment have been a living witness to me and to others. But most of all, you have been the greatest example of the *Seekers of His Face*.

Thank you both for my heritage.

Your Daughter

ACKNOWLEDGMENTS

To my husband PATRICK: Words cannot begin to express my gratitude for all of your love, support and help. I could not have accomplished the task set before me if it had not been for your right hand.

DR. CHARLOTTE BAKER, my friend and mentor: Thank you for all of your endless counsel and your painstaking editing. I thank the Father daily for giving me a "Mack truck" with such love, compassion, strength and truth. Thank you for truth.

REV. MYRNA DOIRON, my co-laborer and friend: Your eagle eye is greatly appreciated. Your words of direction are always on time. Thank you for your support and clarity.

DEE BAXTER: Thank you for all of your encouragement and support. You are a true teacher and your insight, revelation and love for God's infallible Word opened to me rivers of truth.

MARTHA ELIZABETH FERGUSON: Thank you for taking my vision of God's chamber (Most Holy Place) and developing it into the reality of pen and ink.

To my congregation, LIVING FOUNTAIN MINISTRY: Through you I have seen God's faithfulness, provision, deliverance, and glory. You are true vessels yielded to His dealings and His presence. You truly are "Seekers of His Face." Thanks for your prayers, your support, love and faithfulness.

Last, but not least, to my children, Seph and Hannah: Though you may be too young to fully understand all that has happened over the past year, I appreciate your understanding when I had to study and type. I count myself blessed to be your mother. May you walk all the days of your life seeking God's face as you do now.

TABLE OF CONTENTS

FOREWORD BY DR. IVERNA TOMPKINS

Every now and then a book that speaks especially for the moment in which we are living finds its way into our hearts. This is just such a book and it will stimulate the reader to seek for the promised *more* by finding the face of God.

FOREWORD BY DR. FUCHSIA T. PICKETT

As one follows the author, Cynthia Duggan, through her book, *Seekers of His Face*, it is evident from the biblical exegesis in the text that she has done her homework in searching and presenting the Scriptures related to seeking God. It is even more evident to the serious reader that she is expressing these truths out of her personal relationship and living reality of the experience of seeking His face.

Cynthia has walked through every truth she presents and found the higher road: the church within the church. She has learned the difference between living in the outer court as a "saved" person and communing with God in the Holy of Holies where His presence is manifest — knowing that it is in the latter, by beholding His face, that we are *"changed from glory to glory."*

During the Charismatic era, it seems, the church was seeking the hand of the Lord continually, asking for what He could and would give us. We were constantly seeking His blessings, gifts, miracles, and all His hand could provide.

It is refreshing to see the church beginning to seek Him alone — His holiness, His character, and communion with Him, becoming true *Seekers of His Face*.

FOREWORD BY DR. CHARLOTTE BAKER

This books is not for the casual reader who seeks only to be entertained and not challenged. *Seekers of His Face* brings into clear focus the deep heartwrenching cry which is to be found in many of God's people today – *"that I may know Him."*

In this hour, God, by His Spirit, has swept over the Body of Christ with a wonderful wave of renewal, restoration and refreshing. This move, great as it is, is not an end in itself, but rather a preparation for something much greater – the revelation of God Himself to the Church, His Bride. God is drawing unto Himself those who will not be content with anything less than His face – who He is.

For six years I have known Cynthia Duggan both as a friend and a mentor. Seldom have I observed more dedication and growth in ministry and Christian graces. The prophetic mantle which rests on her ministry is evident throughout the book, and the seeking heart will find answers here. This is Cynthia's first venture into the field of writing, but I am sure it will not be her last. I highly recommend this book to those who are *Seekers of His Face*. I am sure it will put into words the deepest cry of your heart.

INTRODUCTION

God has sought a relationship with His own people from the beginning. He said, *"Let us make man in our image, after our likeness"* (Genesis 1:26). God's intention was for the crown of His creation to reflect and express His character. His desire has never changed. Even when man disobeyed and ate of *the tree of the knowledge of good and evil,* God still sought communion, fellowship, and relationship with him.

From God's heart, there is a longing that calls His own past the outer court, through the Holy Place and beyond the veil, into the Most Holy Place. God is placing a hunger, which cannot be satisfied by experiences or manifestations, in the hearts of those who seek Him. This hunger will only be gratified by a kiss from His lips: a face-to-face encounter.

It is with great conviction that I write this book. As each day passes, it brings me to a greater awareness of the Father's desire to reveal Himself to us. In revealing Himself to us, He can ultimately be revealed through us, to a hurting and dying world.

A new day is approaching in which there will be signs and wonders as never before. However, it will flow through an awareness which is: *"Christ in you, the hope of glory"* (Colossians 1:27).

For too long believers have looked at His glory as an object, expecting it to drop from Heaven and knock them over. His gifts and anointing have been treated as mere by-products, instead of expressions of His person. His Church has become title conscious, office conscious, and gift conscious. They have forgotten that the real issue isn't who they are, but who they become as they behold *Him*.

There is truly a Church within the Church, two companies, two experiences in God, receiving in different measure. The time has come for believers to enter the Most Holy Place. Enjoying the benefits of God's hand has been fun, but now we must focus our eyes on His face.

His voice has been stirring me. He has called me deeper. Yesterday's commitment won't do. A choice must be made. For those that would obey His heart's call, the prize of knowing Him awaits. Those who refuse to be content with anything less than beholding His face will be called the Bride, the Lamb's wife. That Bride will be made up of the true *Seekers of His Face*.

Cynthia Duggan
Mt. Pleasant, South Carolina

PART I:

TWO
COMPANIES

CHAPTER ONE

THE REVELATION

A nd Elijah came unto all the people, and said, HOW LONG HALT YE BETWEEN TWO OPINIONS? if the LORD be God, follow him: but if Baal, then follow him. And the people answered him not a word. 1 Kings 18:21

It has been several years ago now, but it seems like yesterday. I was ministering to a group of people when God gave me a question to ask: "Will you run, be a spectator or commit?" The question made a great impact on me personally, for I felt, coupled with it, an overwhelming sense of decision. Even though I had spoken the word myself, I was shaken to the very core. For several minutes afterward I stood, speechless and overwhelmed. I soon found myself prostrate on the floor in repentance and felt like the prophet Isaiah, when he responded to God, *"I am a man of unclean lips."* In the sight of God's holiness, he had felt *"undone."*

When I was able to stand, after what seemed like forever, I noticed that I was not alone in my response. To my surprise, others present were on their faces in God's holy presence.

As the word of the Lord burned within me, I felt the revelation of two companies ignite. Perhaps I had seen it previously – in types, shadows, and patterns from God's

13

Word – but until that particular moment, it had never been so real, so vivid, to me.

I felt the weight of separation. The gulf was vast. I knew that God wanted all believers to be one people, His Son's Bride, but the plumb line between the uncommitted and the heartbound was being drawn. The clarity of the message penetrated my heart just as it had been declared by John in his Revelation:

> *I know thy works, that THOU ART NEITHER COLD NOR HOT: I would thou wert cold or hot. So then because thou art lukewarm, and neither cold nor hot, I will spue thee out of my mouth.*   Revelation 3:15-16

God's message is the same for both leaders and laymen. He is cutting through the intents of our hearts and judging all areas of our commitment (see Hebrews 4:12).

Elijah, God's prophet, saw the division of two companies when he challenged Israel: *How long halt ye between two opinions?* (1 Kings 18:21). Two opinions on commitment, when it comes to our relationship with God is one opinion too many.

I believe God's message is clear. He is shaking His Church, measuring every level of commitment. He is asking serious questions and desires committed responses. We as a Church, a body, cannot walk loosely or aimlessly any longer.

Paul wrote to the Romans:

> *And that, knowing the time, that now it is high time to awake out of sleep: for now is our salvation nearer than when we believed. The night is far spent, the day is at hand: let us therefore cast off the works of darkness, and let us put on the armour of light. Let us walk honestly, as in the*

day; not in rioting and drunkenness, not in chambering and wantonness, not in strife and envying. But put ye on the Lord Jesus Christ, and make not provision for the flesh, to fulfil the lusts thereof. Romans 13:11-14

The definition of two companies is not one that we can arrive at lightly, but it is to be found within the volume of the Sacred Scriptures. There are two distinct companies, and every believer belongs to one or the other. I'm not talking about saved and unsaved, but rather two companies of believing Christians. Those who stay near the throne make up the one company, and the other is composed of those who worship God from afar. Which company do you belong to? What is your response to God's call for commitment? That response alone will be the determining factor.

If you choose to ignore the divine call and continue to walk far from God's throne, don't be surprised if one day you find yourself shut out of the wedding feast. And that is a dangerous risk to take. God gives us the choice, and makes the very best available to us, but He doesn't force us to choose. The choice is ours.

Some governments guarantee certain freedoms for the governed. Within that mandate, an individual may have a certain freedom of choice. But the concept of "choice" has nothing to do with movements, philosophies, or governments. Choice is a God-given privilege.

Every individual, made in the image and likeness of God, can freely come to Him, or can just as easily walk away from His grace. And a person's degree of commitment will ultimately determine his or her capacity to abide in Christ.

Jesus invites every man and woman to come to Him and to walk in the fullness of His Word, of His promises and of His inheritance. Unfortunately, not everyone embraces that offer.

Jesus gave a beautiful illustration of His invitation in the Parable of the Ten Virgins:

> *Then shall the kingdom of heaven be likened unto ten virgins, which took their lamps, and went forth to meet the bridegroom. And five of them were wise, and five were foolish. They that were foolish took their lamps, and took no oil with them: But the wise took oil in their vessels with their lamps. While the bridegroom tarried, they all slumbered and slept. And at midnight there was a cry made, Behold, the bridegroom cometh; go ye out to meet him.*
>
> *Then all those virgins arose, and trimmed their lamps. And the foolish said unto the wise, Give us of your oil; for our lamps are gone out.*
>
> *But the wise answered, saying, Not so; lest there be not enough for us and you: but go ye rather to them that sell, and buy for yourselves.*
>
> *And while they went to buy, the bridegroom came; and they that were ready went in with him to the marriage: and the door was shut.*
>
> *Afterward came also the other virgins, saying, Lord, Lord, open to us.*
>
> *BUT HE ANSWERED AND SAID, VERILY I SAY UNTO YOU, I KNOW YOU NOT.*
>
> *Watch therefore, for ye know neither the day nor the hour wherein the Son of man cometh.*   Matthew 25:1-13

Five of the "virgins" were said to be "wise" and the other five were said to be "foolish." All ten received the same invitation and the same instruction – prepare. The five who were foolish chose not to prepare fresh oil for their lamps, but to depend on what they already had. So, when the time came for the wedding ceremony to begin and the bridegroom called for everyone to come inside, those who had prepared were able to enter and to enjoy the wedding feast, while those who had not prepared were left outside.

The implication of the parable is that there may be "virgins" (Christians) who simply don't make it into the marriage feast. Could these two companies of "virgins" represent the same two companies that God so vividly presented to me – one near the throne and the other far from it?

The first company, those who approach God from a distance, are content when Jesus comes just inside their door. They dare not spend much time with Him, and they don't know Him intimately. They only know Him by what He does, or has done, in their lives. They praise Him for past deeds, but they haven't worshiped Him for Who He is. They look for evidence that He has been around, and expect His works, but they haven't sought His divine nature.

Before they worship Him as Provider, they expect Him to provide. Before they worship Him as Healer, they expect Him to heal. They are content to read about Him, or to feed at His table, but allowing His words to penetrate and change them would require too much time, too much sacrifice. By reason of choice, they are content on the fringes. Involvement, acceptance of God's invitation to draw near, would require their will to be subordinate to His own. And they are unwilling to pay that great a price.

Those who make up the second company are not content on the fringes. They are not content merely having Jesus enter their door. They strive to know Him, to know every part of His nature and character. They seek to know His heart, His will, and His ways. From their innermost being they call out, "Not my will, but thine, be done. Deal with me, penetrate me, change me."

They implore God, "Let Your finger write upon my heart. Let Your desires become mine. Let Your ways become my ways. Let Your character be molded in me and reflected from me."

These true worshipers of God desire only to enter His presence and remain there. They are not thinking of things for Him to *do*. God isn't their servant, but rather they are His. He doesn't need to be doing anything for them. They don't need to hear Him continually speak. They love Him. They worship Him. They've counted the cost and have chosen to press in and to be found *in Him*.

Two companies, two distinct groups, two experiences in God, and two very different measures.

God does not and will not withhold Himself from those who seek Him. He gives Himself to those who seek Him in the same degree that they strive after Him. How much they receive of God is up to them. The veil of the Temple has been rent, but how closely we approach the Most Holy Place is our choice. God will not force any of us into a relationship. He only gives the invitation.

The book of Revelation is filled with colorful imagery. Admittedly, it is difficult to study and, at the very least, confusing. But it is also filled with monumental promise, and each time I read it I find fresh insight.

I see the Heavenly Throne and the Sanctuary, places filled with sound, color, beauty, and worship both by day and by night. Beautiful angels are present; elders, saints, and beasts, each one having specific duties; and voices and their messages. Revelation also foretells a wedding, a union, and a communion. It gives a prophetic illustration of Christ's Bride, the inner company of which we speak. And it says, "*[She] hath made herself ready!*"

The Revelation

*Let us be glad and rejoice, and give honour to him: for the
marriage of the Lamb is come, and HIS WIFE HATH
MADE HERSELF READY. And to her was granted that
she should be arrayed in fine linen, clean and white: for the
fine linen is the righteousness of saints.*

Revelation 19:7-8

The bride's wardrobe is *"fine linen, clean and white,"* and
that *"fine linen"* is her own righteousness — not self-righteousness, but the righteousness she has received from
the Righteous One. Self-righteousness is nothing more
than *"filthy rags,"* but true righteousness is the product of
living in God's grace.

Those who keep their garments will be ready for the
wedding, just as the wise virgins who prepared their
lamps and were ready for the midnight call. Those who
are not properly adorned, however, will be denied entrance.

Perhaps the reason that more *"virgins"* don't choose to
prepare their lamps or keep their garments is that it isn't
cheap. It costs a life on *the way of holiness* of which Isaiah
spoke (Isaiah 35:8).

All of us are "called" to walk in that way:

*And he saith unto me, Write, Blessed are they which are
CALLED unto the marriage supper of the Lamb.*

Revelation 19:9

*And the Spirit and the bride say, Come. And let him that
heareth say, Come. And let him that is athirst come. And
WHOSOEVER WILL, let him take the water of life freely.*

Revelation 22:17

Although *"whosoever will"* is invited, however, it is clear
that not all the called *will take the water of life.* If the Par-

able of the Virgins is any indicator, about half of all professing Christians will fail to make it to the well.

Of those who are called, how many will fill their lamps with fresh oil? Those are questions we must leave with God. The important thing, however, is your personal response. Will you be ready to meet the Bridegroom?

John wrote of the Bride:

> *And there came unto me one of the seven angels which had the seven vials full of the seven last plagues, and talked with me, saying, Come hither, I WILL SHEW THEE THE BRIDE, THE LAMB'S WIFE. And he carried me away in the spirit to a great and high mountain, and shewed me that great city, the holy Jerusalem, descending out of heaven from God, Having the glory of God: and HER light was like unto a stone most precious, even like a jasper stone, clear as crystal;* Revelation 21:9-11

The Bride is unique in her beauty and John described her as a marvelously embellished and radiant city.

She is no stranger to her Heavenly Bridegroom. She has made the necessary preparations and taken time to know her Beloved. She waits in humble elegance for Him to measure her gates with His *"golden reed"* (Verse 15).

When it is time, He will measure her foundation to see if it is properly established. He will check the dimension of her walls to see the perfection of her beauty, and her pillars to see her strength. He will prove her stairs to see the depths of her truth, and He will examine her windows to see if she lets in the light of revelation, and if she allows it to reflect. He will look into her chambers to see if she has enlarged them for Him to dwell therein. He will review her gates to see if they are open to Him (see Ezekiel 40 and Revelation 11).

The Revelation

After He has throuroughly inspected the Bride's city, He will declare that it *is "granted that she should be arrayed in fine linen, clean and white."* Having witnessed the Bride, graced and embellished, John is compelled to write: *"Blessed are they which are called unto the marriage supper of the Lamb."*

Still, God gives everyone the same opportunity. He calls all. It is the degree of our personal response that will determine the depth of our walk in the fullness of His promise.

In speaking of the two companies, I would not want to further divide the Church. We have enough separation, judgment and criticism in the Body of Christ already. My goal is to present a mark or goal of holiness, and to encourage every believer to press toward it. That goal is the likeness of Christ.

Several years ago I was ministering, sharing a message entitled, "God Will Measure His Temple," when I heard the Spirit say, "I've moved in, and I'm having a garage sale." I chuckled to myself, until I realized exactly what God was calling for. He was saying that we needed a good house cleaning and that we should place a large sign out front saying, "Everything Must Go!"

As a collector and "saver" of old things, I realized that the Spirit was telling me to "lighten my load." Before God could measure my temple, I would need to get rid of old hurts, frustrations, disappointments, and traditions.

It sounds easy, but those who have actually done the house cleaning know that it is not as easy as it sounds. It hurts to get rid of our old relics of self. For me, it was one of the most painful spring cleanings I ever experienced. But I needed it. A Holy Spirit house cleaning will sweep away the clutter from our lives, clean us up and establish us in the reality of the psalmist's words:

Seekers of His Face

The Lord is the portion of mine inheritance.   Psalm 16:5

Living close to God's throne requires that we pay a price and that we make a commitment. What is your decision?

Let us now look at several Bible characters to see what their decision was and to establish the foundation for two companies. As we see the types, shadows, and patterns of Scripture, we will learn much. No image is perfect or complete, but such revelation shows the heart of God and leads to the Most Holy Place where Seekers of His Face cast themselves down before His presence.

CHAPTER TWO

TWO BROTHERS: CAIN AND ABEL

*A*nd Adam knew Eve his wife; and she conceived,
and bare Cain, and said, I have gotten a man from
the LORD. And she again bare his brother Abel.
*And Abel was a keeper of sheep, but Cain was a tiller of the
ground. And in process of time it came to pass, that Cain
brought of the fruit of the ground an offering unto the
LORD. And Abel, he also brought of the firstlings of his
flock and of the fat thereof. And the LORD had respect unto
Abel and to his offering:* Genesis 4:1-5

Just a few pages into the book of Genesis, we find a
vivid illustration of two companies. The first two brothers were very different. For one thing they had different
professions. Cain was a farmer, *"a tiller of the ground,"* and
Abel was *"a keeper of sheep."* The two sons of Adam and
Eve are examples of two companies in the respect of their
relationship to God and their resulting obedience or disobedience. Even though they may not be a complete or
perfect type in themselves, they do help us determine how
God views disobedience in relationship to His laws and
principles.

We don't know the entire history of their lives, but the
phrase *"in the process of time"* indicates that there was a
time for both brothers to make offerings to the Lord. Cain

brought his offering of *"the firstfruits of the ground."* Abel brought *"of the firstlings of his flock."* So each of the brothers presented an offering to the Lord from the fruits of his own labor. This would seem to be in order.

But there were some problems. One of those problems was that a curse had come upon the ground as a result of the disobedience of Adam and Eve. Therefore anything coming from the ground was also cursed, making it an unacceptable sacrifice.

Surely Adam and Eve had taught their sons concerning sacrifice. After all, they had experienced disobedience and had suffered the consequences. One thing they could never forget was that God had provided, through the sacrifice of animals, skins with which they could cover themselves. They understood sacrifice.

Cain had to know that he was doing something unacceptable to God, for a just God would not have otherwise held him responsible.

It is very possible that, like so many other young men, Cain was simply rebelling against his parents and their instruction. But, whatever the case, it is clear that he was rebelling and, therefore, God could not accept his sacrifice.

We can be sure that Adam and Eve taught their boys God's principles, many of which they had learned the hard way themselves. They understood God's word and knew there was a consequence to disobedience. They knew they had a responsibility toward maintaining relationship, communion and, ultimately, God's glory.

So Cain knew what he was doing, and thus was deliberately disobeying God. Abel acted in obedience. Cain refused to believe that his offering from his own crops could be any less appreciated than his brother's lambs.

In presenting an offering from the ground, Cain was making five fatal mistakes. 1. He was refusing the instruction of his parents. 2. He was insisting on approaching God based on his own worthiness instead of doing it God's way. 3. He was presenting a product of the cursed ground instead of an offering that required the shedding of blood. 4. He was presuming that he had an automatic relationship with the Lord, which he didn't. 5. He was brazenly assuming that God was obligated to accept his sacrifice, which He wasn't.

Cain's life is an example of the destruction that can come when we fail to maintain a proper relationship with God and fail to offer Him a proper sacrifice. He ignored the counsel of God, to his own hurt.

Abel obeyed his parents and the Lord's command they taught him and learned to walk in faith. It earned him a place in "Faith's Hall of Fame":

> *By faith Abel offered unto God a more excellent sacrifice than Cain, by which he obtained witness that he was righteous, God testifying of his gifts: and by it he being dead yet speaketh.* Hebrews 11:4

Adam had communed with God and walked with Him in the cool of the day. He had known God's voice. Able took all this by faith. He had only his parents' testimony that it was true, for the physical Paradise was hidden from him. Yet he believed, without seeing, and that made him one of faith's heroes.

The life of Cain, however, stands as an example of God's judgment for disobedience in relationship and sacrifice. Abel, by bringing a "firstling from the flock," obeyed the instructions of his parents and approached God, not on the basis of his own righteousness, but on the basis of sacrifice, the blood. We cannot approach God by any other sacrifice. The prophet Isaiah declared that

He *"hath borne our griefs and carried our sorrows."* He *"was wounded for our transgressions, he was bruised for our iniquities."* He was *"oppressed, and he was afflicted, yet he opened not his mouth: he is brought as a lamb to the slaughter"* (Isaiah 53:4-5 and 7).

Those who have joined Abel's company stand on God's Word. They press in to know Him and be found in Him, obedient to all His ways.

Both brothers had the same opportunity, but they were unmistakably different in their responses to God and His instruction. And, from the wall of response, God drops His plumb line. Those who respond as Cain are found to be out of plumb, bowed and bent; they are useless to the Kingdom. The New Jerusalem, the Lamb's Bride, is a marvelous edifice, a glorious city, and, in its building, nothing that is out of plumb can be used. Only those who stand straight beside God's plumb line are ready for the Master Builder, the Carpenter from Galilee. He can place them in His heavenly edifice with no fear that they will cause a structural failure.

As Able brought a more excellent sacrifice, by faith, the company that he represents walks in faith. They walk in relationship and awareness of the indwelling of Christ, the *"hope of glory"* (Colossians 1:27). This makes them reflectors of God's glory:

> *Arise, shine; for thy light is come, and the glory of the LORD is risen upon thee. For, behold, the darkness shall cover the earth, and gross darkness the people: but the LORD shall arise upon thee, and HIS GLORY SHALL BE SEEN UPON THEE.*   Isaiah 60:1-2

Abel's company reflects His light. Jesus said, *"I am the light,"* (John 8:12). He gives the light that Abel's company

26

reflects, the light that they bear in darkness (Hebrews 1:3). Relationship with Jesus and the manifestation of His character and nature make Abel's company reflectors of God's light and His glory.

Recently this principle's truth came alive for me. It was during a Sunday service, and as I started worshiping, I heard the Spirit speak, "What you behold, you become." I felt a hot iron pierce my eyes, and as I stood in God's presence, the Spirit impressed the following on my heart:

> *But we all, with open face beholding as in a glass the glory of the Lord, ARE CHANGED INTO THE SAME IMAGE FROM GLORY TO GLORY, even as by the Spirit of the Lord.* 2 Corinthians 3:18

In worship we come before Him, and it is in worship that we behold Him, and there, in His presence, the Spirit does His sovereign work. It's like the transformation of a caterpillar into a beautiful butterfly.

I've often pondered the Scripture *"be ye holy; for I am holy"* (1 Peter 1:16) with a degree of uncertainty. What a tall order! But now, in the light of this revelation, it is an obtainable goal. The Spirit's revelation had shown me that I would become what I beheld, what I looked into. I'll be transformed into His image and likeness. This transformation doesn't depend on me. Only *He* can do that work. It depends solely on His person, Who He is. So, walking in relationship will make us like the One we are looking to and worshiping.

It has been said that husbands and wives start to look alike after they've been married for a number of years. If we are really part of Christ's Bride, then we'll start looking like Him. But just as a relationship between husband and wife is a difficult thing to maintain (once the honeymoon is over), so too our relationship with the Lord. It takes work to keep the relationship alive. There is a price to be paid.

Some married couples go through life without working to maintain their relationship. They go on, day after day, without seeking each other out. They are deceiving themselves, and one day — suddenly, as if it happened overnight — they will find themselves without a relationship. That same thing happens when Christians don't nurture their relationship with the Lord.

Adam and Eve learned the hard way, through disobedience, that there is a price to be paid to maintain God's glory in our lives. In a deliberate and foolish act they ate of the forbidden tree and, as a result, found themselves naked, stripped of God's covering.

Abel remembered that lesson, and the company he represents has learned to pay attention to the Lord's instruction and has willingly learned to walk in truth, maintaining itself in relationship with the Lord. Members of Abel's company have found that by paying the price of obedience and maintaining the proper relationship with God, they can walk in His glory. They have learned that God's glory is not some spooky little cloud; it is a Person, Himself, and not a thing.

When Moses was on the back side of the desert, he saw a burning bush and the Spirit of the Lord told him to take off his shoes because the ground on which he stood was holy. This command had nothing to do with the type of dirt found in that area, or the type of bush that seemed to be on fire. It came because of a the Person who was there, manifested in that place.

How often we jump in and out of prayer lines and look to Heaven as if God's glory should fall upon us, knock us down and we will walk around glowing. I realize that I

Two Brothers: Cain and Abel

may be exaggerating, but I hope to make a point. If our idea of glory rests on some "glowing" anointing, then we will probably miss one of the greatest outpourings of God's Spirit that the Church has ever seen. When we consider the glory of God in such terms (everything glowing), seeking an experience and not a person, then we probably won't show any responsibility or accountability towards that glory. However, if we totally commit ourselves to His person, as part of Abel's company, we will never go about as individuals who take no responsibility for their actions and utterances.

As I was growing up, a popular comedic personality by the name of Flipp Wilson was always blaming the devil for his own mischief and base jokes. "The devil made me do it," he was fond of saying. It seems that, for some who pretend to be part of Abel's company, the reverse may be true. They say, "It was the anointing that made me do that," or "It was the Holy Spirit." How easily they seem to blame God's Spirit for their own fleshly outbursts! As a result, many churches and leaders despise the prophetic stirring of our time. Today's church is witnessing a genuine move of the prophetic, but it must come through vessels who will accept responsibility and be accountable before man and before God for their ministries. Such are those who belong to Abel's company.

Cain's company has heard the counsel of God but, for the most part, continues to ignore it. Let us choose to draw near and know God.

CHAPTER THREE

TWO COMPANIES WITHIN THE LEVITICAL PRIESTHOOD

*N**ow therefore, if ye will obey my voice indeed, and keep my covenant, then ye shall be a peculiar treasure unto me above all people: for all the earth is mine: And ye shall be unto me A KINGDOM OF PRIESTS, AND AN HOLY NATION. These are the words which thou shalt speak unto the children of Israel.*

Exodus 19:5-6

Perhaps the one place where the division of two companies would be least expected is among God's priesthood.

As this passage from Exodus shows us, God's heart has always been for a people who would walk in obedience to His covenants and heed His voice. His desire hasn't changed. He's still looking for a kingdom of priests, a holy nation. Peter wrote to the Church:

But ye are A CHOSEN GENERATION, A ROYAL PRIESTHOOD, AN HOLY NATION, A PECULIAR PEOPLE; that ye should shew forth the praises of him who hath called you out of darkness into his marvellous light:

1 Peter 2:9

God has called us to be *a chosen generation*, a generation that will be holy and peculiar and that will *"shew forth [His] praises."*

What isn't immediately apparent is the true meaning of being a priest before God. Generally, people see the beauty of position, the prestige so often associated with leadership in the church (even if this prestige is more imagined than real). What is harder to see is that being a priest of God demands responsibility. Keeping His temple pure and without defilement isn't easy. It isn't always fun. It rarely, if ever, makes the flesh happy. Paul wrote:

> *And what agreement hath the temple of God with idols? for ye are the temple of the living God; as God hath said, I will dwell in them, and walk in them; and I will be their God, and they shall be my people. WHEREFORE COME OUT FROM AMONG THEM, AND BE YE SEPARATE, saith the Lord, and touch not the unclean thing; and I will receive you,* 2 Corinthians 6:16-17

Those who would walk holy, separate and peculiar must do so in *His* strength. And they will not find the life of leadership nearly as glamorous as they might have imagined. The company of priests who would walk separate was birthed in the very heart of God. During Israel's long journey though the wilderness, God instructed Moses regarding His people's government. Israel, until that time, had not been governed by God's law, but by the harshness of her taskmasters. In Egypt, the people of Israel had known only a life of burdens and afflictions, but God now had a new way of life for them. He called them to a life of liberty and freedom, a life of fellowship and relationship. God relayed His heart's desire to Moses in the form of seven "I wills":

Two Companies Within the Levitical Priesthood

Wherefore say unto the children of Israel, I am the LORD, and I WILL bring you out from under the burdens of the Egyptians, and I WILL rid you out of their bondage, and I WILL redeem you with a stretched out arm, and with great judgments: And I WILL take you to me for a people, and I WILL be to you a God: and ye shall know that I am the LORD your God, which bringeth you out from under the burdens of the Egyptians. And I WILL bring you in unto the land, concerning the which I did swear to give it to Abraham, to Isaac, and to Jacob; and I WILL give it you for an heritage: I am the LORD. Exodus 6:6-8

God fully intended to bring His people into complete freedom, relationship, provision and inheritance. He sought to be more than a deliverer for His people. He wanted to be their Redeemer, their Father, their Lord and, above all else, He sought to be their personal God, living with them and within them. God used Moses to deliver them and bring them out of the land of bondage.

But God had another role for Moses to play. He was to be God's prophet and lawgiver, teaching God's people His laws and His ways. Therefore, God gave him two tablets of stone with His laws written upon them in ten commandments. These Ten Commandments have two portions. The first four commandments govern our relationship with God, and the last six deal with human relationships.

God also spoke to Moses about a place for Him to dwell, sacrifices that the people should make to Him, and a priesthood that would minister to Him in holiness. Every word of God's instruction was specific. Everything was to be done according to His plan, for there was a promise of redemption hidden in each item of the Tabernacle and its function. Later we will investigate this further.

God set apart the people of the tribe of Levi to be His priests, and as priests they were to be His outstretched hand to the people and His ministers before the altar, the table and the ark – which served as His throne.

As a priest of God, we too are called to be God's outstretched hands. For believers today, the priesthood is not an office of ceremonial works, but has more to do with revelation and relationship, partaking of Christ and thus bringing to life every type and shadow offered by Aaron's priesthood to a dying world.

In Aaron's priesthood, each priest held specific duties related to their genealogy. Aaron and his sons ministered as high priests. When traveling, specific families, also descendants of Aaron, transported the various parts and furnishings of the wilderness Tabernacle. However, their chief responsibility was to stand as mediators between God and man.

The Apostle Paul taught that though the Body be one, it has many members. The individual members, according to the grace that is upon them, completes their own operation (see Romans 12:3). As God's priests, we accomplish our roles, by the grace that is upon our lives. Together, we stand as God's living Tabernacle.

Since Jesus had not yet made the ultimate sacrifice, the Levites had the responsibility of offering prayers, sacrifices, and intercession to the Lord on behalf of God's people. Additionally, they instructed the people in God's laws. They taught about sacrifices, cleansings, and feasts.

They priests were not permitted to own land (see Numbers 18:20). They had no physical inheritance, as the other tribes did. The Lord alone was to be their portion.

The priests stood as an example to the people. They

taught what was acceptable to the Lord, and they lived it before the people. At least that was the ideal. In time, various members of the Levitical priesthood committed transgressions and abominations. It is here that we begin to see two companies formed within the Levitical system.

Nadab and Abihu, for instance, Aaron's sons, would be remembered for their iniquity. God had instructed Moses in the preparation and use of incense for worship (see Exodus 30:8-9 and 35-38). His instruction was complete, from the specific substances to be used to the precise amounts. Nothing was left to guess work. Any old mix wouldn't do. Repeatedly the word *"sweet"* was used concerning the incense and the *"savour"* of its burning (see Leviticus 6:15).

The use of incense was nothing new. It had been used often in the worship of false gods:

> *Because they have forsaken me, and have burned incense unto other gods, THAT THEY MIGHT PROVOKE ME TO ANGER with all the works of their hands; therefore my wrath shall be kindled against this place, and shall not be quenched.* 2 Kings 22:17

Burning incense *unto other gods* was contrary to God's intention. Priests burnt incense before God to make a pure and sweet aroma in His nostrils.

Nadab and Abihu knew God's laws concerning incense, yet they had to do it their own way. To burn it, they brought their own fire, instead of fire from the altar, as God has instructed. They offered incense at the wrong time and in the wrong place. Their efforts were termed "strange fire," and what they did created a stench in God's nostrils — not *a sweet savour.*

Moses later reported what happened next:

*And there went out fire from the LORD, and devoured
them, and they died before the LORD.*   Leviticus 10:2

God was so offended by the actions of these priests
that He commanded Aaron not to mourn his sons' death
(see Leviticus 10:6). Nadab and Abihu had made three
fatal mistakes: 1. They offered strange fire from unholy
incense (see verse 1). 2. They failed to sanctify themselves
(see verse 3). 3. They failed to glorify the Lord before the
people (see verse 3). And they paid dearly for their mistakes.

In New Testament times, incense takes on a much
deeper meaning:

*And another angel came and stood at the altar, having a
golden censer; and there was given unto him MUCH IN-
CENSE, that he should offer it with the prayers of all saints
upon the golden altar which was before the throne. And
THE SMOKE OF THE INCENSE, which came with the
prayers of the saints, ascended up before God out of the
angel's hand.*   Revelation 8:3-4

New Testament priests no longer offer up physical incense; rather, they have spiritual revelation upon which
to build their understanding of incense and the concepts
it typifies. Today's priests, those who keep themselves
holy and separate, bring prayers mixed with sweet incense before the Lord.

In Moses's day, all the spices that went into making
"the pure incense of sweet spices" were to be processed *"according to the work of the apothecary"* (Exodus 37:29). The
work of the apothecary (a perfumer) was an ancient art.
The apothecary knew how to dip flowers in heated oils
and squeeze or press out the perfume to be used in making incense. His work released fragrant aromas.

Two Companies Within the Levitical Priesthood

Jesus was subjected to violence and duress, pressing and wrenching, through His trials, testings, temptations and sufferings. Yet, from His suffering came forth a divine fragrance. Everything He suffered made Him a sweet aroma to the Father.

Cain came before God in his own righteousness and pride, not having experienced the pressing and wrenching that purges self and brings forth humility. His company must be subjected to the press, and self-will and desire must be wrenched away.

Every person who would find a place near the throne must be subjected to the Master Perfumer's heated oil — boiling Holy Spirit oil — and then squeezed and pressed until a sweet aroma rises into God's nostrils.

The ingredients found in a believer's spiritual incense, rising from a life that has been subjected to the pressure of trials overcome, testing approved, temptations avoided, and sufferings endured, are prayer (see Ephesians 6:18), thanksgiving (see Colossians 4:2) and surrender (see 1 Thessalonians 5:23).

Nabad and Abihu failed to prepare either themselves or their sacrifice, and the result was devastating. God's heart longs for His people to worship Him *"in spirit and in truth"* (John 4:23-24). He wants His people to enter into full and rich relationship with Him and bring properly prepared sacrifices into His Holy Place.

Not long after the judgment of Nabad and Abihu had occurred, there was a massive rebellion against Moses led by a man named Korah:

> *Now Korah, the son of Izhar, the son of Kohath, the son of Levi, ... took men: And they rose up before Moses, with certain of the children of Israel, two hundred and fifty princes of the assembly, famous in the congregation, men of renown:* Numbers 16:1-2

It seems that Korah's problem was that he entertained the idea, *"I can do it better."* The seed of rebellion thus germinated in his heart and he nurtured it. His bitterness affected many others, something the Scriptures warn us against:

> *Looking diligently lest any man fail of the grace of God;*
> *LEST ANY ROOT OF BITTERNESS SPRINGING UP*
> *trouble you, AND THEREBY MANY BE DEFILED;*
> Hebrews 12:15

Korah's hunger for power and authority caused him to rebel against God's leadership choice. This is a common problem in the church and one that has caused much harm. It always harms more than the one having the problem. It harms other individuals, and it harms the entire church.

Thoughts of criticism and feelings of jealousy lead to rebellion, and such rebellion can put down roots and cause *"a root of bitterness,"* a treacherous growth. Solomon warned that envy is *"the rottenness of the bones"* (Proverbs 14:30). If given a chance, rebellion will rot your bones and make you sick, just as it did in the case of Miriam, Moses' sister (see Numbers 12:9-10).

The world today is filled with messages about our "rights." These constantly repeated messages bombard the mind with thoughts that are not spiritual and which corrupt sound thought on the meaning of God's authority. This world's system will not work for the Church. The Church is a living, breathing Body, and Christ is its Head. As such, He is the Ultimate Authority, and He has established order for the exercise of spiritual authority (see Ephesians 4:11).

Korah's attitude led him to rebellion, and believers today must take care not to fall into the same trap. The temptation to rebel, to exercise our "freedom of choice," is an ever-present snare that, with countless other pitfalls, has caused many Christians to fall.

God's ways are not our ways. He searches the very depths of a person's heart, looking beyond external qualifications and seeing internal commitments — the intentions of the heart. No amount of talent, education or wealth will help a person whose heart has been disqualified by sustained rebellion.

God reminded Samuel, the prophet, not to look upon man's outward appearance, when he sought to anoint a new king for Israel:

> *But the LORD said unto Samuel, Look not on his countenance, or on the height of his stature; because I have refused him: for the LORD seeth not as man seeth; for man looketh on the outward appearance, but the LORD looketh ON THE HEART.* 1 Samuel 16:7

In the Church, human ideas of leadership must be swept aside. God's established order for the government of His people is the only one that counts, and any attempt to change that order by human imposition will eventually bring failure.

Moses, upon hearing of Korah's rebellion, grieved and fell on his face before the Lord. The Lord heard his cry and gave him instructions concerning the rebellious ones. Moses told Korah and his followers to come the next day and to bring their censers, so that they could present themselves before the Lord and worship Him. The Lord would choose among them.

The next day, Korah, with two of his best leaders, Dathan and Abiram, came before Moses and the people.

They wanted to govern, and they thought they were about to have their chance. But before they could do anything, Moses was instructed by the Lord to separate himself from the rebellious people. God was about to destroy them. This grieved Moses. He didn't want to see many others suffer for the sins of one man and he pleaded with God not to destroy so many. In response, the Lord instructed him to separate himself from the families of Korah, Dathan, and Abiram. Then, when Moses had finished speaking to the people, the earth opened up and swallowed the rebels and all that pertained to them.

Korah's censers had been filled with pride and rebellion, and these are two characteristics that God rejects. He is looking for humility and submission. Anything less becomes a stench in His nostrils.

God had chosen Aaron, not Korah, and Korah's insistence on taking control could not change God's mind. God doesn't see with eyes of flesh as we do. His way of seeing things isn't limited like ours. He looks at a person's very heart.

Second guessing God's choice, for whatever reason, is the same mistake that Korah made. It is sin, and will be judged accordingly.

God checks the aroma coming from our uplifted censers. If a censer has been lifted presumptuously and strange fire offered, His displeasure is certain, and we place ourselves in danger of His judgment, just as did Cain and Aaron's two sons and Korah.

God is expecting a sweet fragrance to rise from our censers, and in order to keep that bouquet appealing, we must allow no rebellion or pride to enter and spoil its aroma.

Korah's rebellion led not only to his own destruction, but also to the doom of a multitude of others. Rebellion can quickly grow out of control, like a cancer, and can infect the whole Body.

Gossip usually finds its roots in jealousy, hurt, or rebellion. These three enemies, and the talk they inspire, are devastating. They soon lead to lies that even the speaker wouldn't have imagined, causing greater infection. Many have said that "talk is cheap," but cheap talk commonly leads to a costly payment.

I overheard one of my fellow ministers say, while she was ministering on day, "Talk is not cheap. It comes with a great price." The truth of her words penetrated my heart and the heart of many others as well. A dead silence filled the room as many began to understand either the truth she had spoken or the pain of the statement.

The Scriptures warn us:

DEATH AND LIFE ARE IN THE POWER OF THE TONGUE: and they that love it shall eat the fruit thereof.
Proverbs 18:21

This confirms the fact that cheap talk can have devastating effects. Perhaps it is time for the people of God to take what comes out of their mouths more seriously.

Korah's heart was filled with rebellion. He went about from tent to tent contaminating everyone with the words that poured from *"the abundance of his heart,"* sowing rebellion's seeds. And thus he caused many others to suffer. Entertaining gossip and rebellion often makes the participants guilty by association. In this case, the penalty was severe – death.

The Scriptures record other incidents that illustrate what happened to the distant company within Levi's descendants. One such episode centers around Eli, another high priest of Israel, and his two sons, Hophni and Phinehas. These sons were profoundly evil (see 1 Samuel 2:12) and were known to lie with women in the door of the Tabernacle.

Hophni and Phinehas were also greedy. As priests, they were permitted to take a certain portion of each sacrifice for their own food, but they used a special hook to dip into the pot and take out more than their portion. They were not satisfied with enough, they wanted more than enough. The two men also took from the raw meat the Lord's portion of the fat. This greatly offended the Lord.

Although he heard reports of his sons' behavior, Eli was either unable or unwilling to take action against them. He compromised to keep peace in the family and neglected his sons' discipline, and because of this, the Lord cut off his house. In one day, his sons were killed at the hands of the Philistines. This was a fulfillment of prophecy:

And there came a man of God unto Eli, and said unto him, Thus saith the LORD, ... And this shall be a sign unto thee, that shall come upon thy two sons, on Hophni and Phinehas; in one day they shall die both of them.

1 Samuel 2:27 and 34

In time, the Philistines also took the sacred Ark of the Covenant. When Eli heard about this, he fell off his stool backward, broke his neck, and died:

And the messenger answered and said, Israel is fled before the Philistines, and there hath been also a great slaughter among the people, and thy two sons also, Hophni and Phinehas, are dead, and the ark of God is taken. And it came to pass, when he made mention of the ark of God, that he fell from off the seat backward by the side of the gate, and his

Two Companies Within the Levitical Priesthood

*neck brake, and he died: for he was an old man, and heavy.
And he had judged Israel forty years.*

1 Samuel 4:17-18

There were indeed many discouraging incidents surrounding the Levitical priesthood, but God had a promise
for His people:

*And I will raise me up a faithful priest, that shall do ac-
cording to that which is in mine heart and in my mind:
and I will build him a sure house; and HE SHALL WALK
BEFORE MINE ANOINTED FOR EVER.*

1 Samuel 2:35

Both Samuel and Zadok (whom we will examine in
the next chapter) partially fulfill this prophecy. Some say
that Christ perfectly completed it. The *"faithful priest"* of
which this prophecy speaks was to *"walk before [the Lord's]
anointed for ever."* This reference to *"[the Lord's] anointed"*
is very likely a reference to Jesus Himself and, if that is
true, perhaps the priest spoken of by this prophecy is the
Church. I believe that God is raising up a faithful priesthood today that will do according to that which is in His
heart and mind. This priesthood will do God's biding regardless of programs, schedules, or agendas.

To make up part of this priesthood, He is looking for
individuals who have counted the cost and are willing to
pay the price. He seeks a people that is convinced that
the ultimate reward is worth the ultimate sacrifice.

CHAPTER FOUR

A FAITHFUL PRIESTHOOD

*I*t shall be for the priests that are sanctified of the
sons of Zadok; which have kept my charge,
which went not astray when the children of Israel went
astray, as the Levites went astray.   Ezekiel 48:11

Zadok, also a descendant of Aaron, was a priest who
walked in faithfulness before the Lord, even in the face
of a great rebellion. He was a high priest under King
David and served with Abiathar, a descendant of Eli.

Abiathar had joined David in the wilderness of Ziklag
and faithfully served him there, despite the fact that he
had not yet become king. Samuel had anointed him for
the position, but his time had not yet come. In time, King
Saul was killed in battle, and then David was elevated to
kingship.

During David's reign, Israel won many victories, but
he committed two sins that would undermine his suc-
cesses — adultery and murder. As a result, God sent the
prophet Nathan to pronounce judgment upon him and
his house:

*And the LORD sent Nathan unto David. And he came
unto him, and said unto him, There were two men in one
city; the one rich, and the other poor. The rich man had
exceeding many flocks and herds: But the poor man had*

*nothing, save one little ewe lamb, which he had bought and
nourished up: and it grew up together with him, and with
his children; it did eat of his own meat, and drank of his
own cup, and lay in his bosom, and was unto him as a
daughter. And there came a traveller unto the rich man,
and he spared to take of his own flock and of his own herd,
to dress for the wayfaring man that was come unto him;
but took the poor man's lamb, and dressed it for the man
that was come to him. And David's anger was greatly kindled against the man; and he said to Nathan, As the LORD
liveth, the man that hath done this thing shall surely die:
And he shall restore the lamb fourfold, because he did this
thing, and because he had no pity. And Nathan said to
David, Thou art the man.*   2 Samuel 12:1-7*

Partial fulfillment of this prophecy came through one
of David's sons, Adonijah, who desired to be king in his
father's stead (1 Kings 1:5-7). David had aged by then,
and his fourth son began to believe that it might be easy
to dethrone him and take his place. He conspired with
Joab, the commander-in-chief of Israel's army, and Abiathar, one of the high priests, to help him gain the throne.

Nathan heard about the conspiracy and told Bathsheba,
the queen. And together they informed David of the conspiracy.

When David knew what his son was planning to do,
he got together Nathan the prophet, Zadok the other high
priest, and Solomon his son. They took the horn of anointing oil and anointed Solomon as king and the rebellion
was quickly ended.

Because of his association and participation with
Adonijah's rebellion, Abiathar deserved death, but Solomon spared his life because of the faithfulness he had
demonstrated to his father David in the wilderness and
because of his loyalty during Absalom's rebellion. Nev-

ertheless, the new king stripped Abiathar of his priestly duties and position, thus fulfilling the prophecy given to Eli years before in Shiloh.

In the case of Adonijah's rebellion and defeat, we find at least two cases of the fathers' sins being visited upon the children. David's sin was visited upon Adonijah, and Eli's negligence was imposed upon Abiathar.

Adonijah had conducted himself like a proud peacock. He *"prepared him chariots and horsemen, and fifty men to run before him"* (1 King 1:5). For this reason, it wasn't easy to have much sympathy for him when the tide turned. Yet, with defeat and humiliation, his behavior failed to improve, and there was no sign of repentance in him.

Abiathar's case was equally sad. We can only imagine what caused him to rebel against David after a life of long and consecrated service to his king. It is heart wrenching for me to image the impact that this judgment must have had on him. It brought shame upon him and took away everything that his life had been.

Abiathar must have felt abandoned by God, and that must have been a living death. He had no promise or assurance, to which to hold. The only thing left for him was a bitter reality of lost relationships. Everywhere he went I'm sure there were people whispering, "There goes a man who was once the high priest." But he had rebelled against God and against God's servants and had distanced himself from the inner court of relationship.

God's heart is for His priests to walk daily in the reality of a relationship with Him, not in having been, "back then," in step with God. Abiathar, after having lived so many years in God's blessing, would now bare the scars of his lost relationship.

And he was not unique. Many are scarred in their relationship and have lost their way. How sad. Rather than carry the scars of defeat, God wants us to carry the mark of a living, breathing, fellowship with our Lord.

Perhaps Abiathar has a strike against him by being a descendant of Eli, for Eli's priesthood is an example of ministry according to the flesh. Happily there is another model, Zadok's faithful priesthood:

Zadok was a descendant of Eleazar, one of Aaron's sons (see 2 Samuel 8:17 and 1 Chronicles 24:3). His name means *just, justified,* or *righteous.* We know very little about him, but we do know that he was faithful to David until the very end, even when serving the king was no longer popular. And through this faithful priest God chose to establish "a sure house."

There was a prophecy given to Phinehas, the son of Eleazar, the son of Aaron. That prophecy is recorded in Numbers 25:6-13. In it God made a covenant of an everlasting priesthood with Phinehas. Except for a brief interruption, when Eli's house served, every high priest from Phinehas's time until 70 AD was his descendant. Further, Zadok was a descendant of Phinehas.

Some may think that the Lord didn't keep His promise to Phinehas concerning an *"everlasting"* priesthood. In 70 AD the Levitical priesthood was terminated because of a crushing Roman victory over Israel. Phinehas'and Zadok's descendants, are mentioned again in the prophetic Word:

> *But the priests the Levites, the sons of Zadok, that kept the charge of my sanctuary when the children of Israel went astray from me, they shall come near to me to minister unto me, and they shall stand before me to offer unto me the fat and the blood, saith the Lord GOD: They shall enter into my sanctuary, and they shall come near to my table, to minister unto me, and they shall keep my charge.*
> Ezekiel 44:15,16

God took Ezekiel, in a vision, to a very high mountain.

A Faithful Priesthood

There the prophet saw something that resembled a city. He also saw a man whose appearance was *"like brass."* This sounds very similar to other presentations of Christ in a posture of judgment (see Revelation 1:15 and 2:18). In the Scriptures, brass often stands for judgment. This man, whose appearance was *"like brass,"* seems to have been the Lord Himself. In His hand was *"a line of flax"* and *"a measuring reed."* At this point the Lord told Ezekiel to mark well what he saw.

There were three courts: an outer court, an inner court and a sanctuary. Each court consisted of gates, stairs, windows, pillars and chambers. In these places, Ezekiel saw a vision of the priesthood and its function in relation to each of the three courts.

Today our Judge stands, judging our chambers. He judges our gates to see if we have given Him access to every area of our lives. He judges our stairs to see how far we have climbed in the things of God. He checks to see if we have stopped on the first stair, and are no longer seeking Him, content with just one revelation. He checks to see if we have gone on to receive the full knowledge and revelation of the Word (see Hebrews 5:13-14). He also measures our windows to see if we have let the light of revelation in and the light of relationship out. He checks our pillars to see where our strength rests and our chambers to see what they contain.

In the vision, God brought Ezekiel back to the outer gate of the sanctuary and told him to *mark well* everything he saw there (see Ezekiel 44:5). It was then that the Lord said to His prophet:

> *In that ye have brought into my sanctuary strangers, uncircumcised in heart, and uncircumcised in flesh, to be in my sanctuary, to pollute it, even my house, when ye offer my bread, the fat and the blood, and they have broken my*

*covenant because of all your abominations. AND YE
HAVE NOT KEPT THE CHARGE OF MINE HOLY
THINGS: but ye have set keepers of my charge in my sanctuary for yourselves. Thus saith the Lord GOD; No
stranger, uncircumcised in heart, nor uncircumcised in
flesh, shall enter into my sanctuary, of any stranger that is
among the children of Israel. And the Levites that are gone
away far from me, when Israel went astray, which went
astray away from me after their idols; they shall even bear
their iniquity.*   Ezekiel 44:7-10

God is holy. Everything He touches must be holy, and
everything that touches Him must be holy.

In this vision, God's statues, ordinances, and laws concerning His House and what He expected of His ministering priests was detailed. Sin and improper adminis-
tration of God's House by a carnal priesthood that had
neglected the things of God led to a divine division of the
Levitical priesthood. God dropped a plumb line, and those
whose priestly service did not conform to true plumb –
those who were bent, twisted, and in danger of collapse
– were separated from those who stood upright and offered holy sacrifices to their righteous God.

Those priests who ministered before idols, causing the
House of Israel to fall away from the worship of Jehovah,
would bear the punishment of their sins. They were given
charge over the gates of the house and enjoined to slay
animals for burnt offerings and to sacrifice them. They
were not, however, allowed to minister before the Lord
in the office of priest. They could no longer go near the
holy things in the Most Holy Place. They were to bear
their shame and abomination before the people. They
were keepers of the house, nothing more.

Zadok's company was upright, squared and plumbed.
They had kept charge of the Lord's House when the other

priests had gone astray. They had been obedient to their divine commission, keeping the sanctuary and coming near to the Lord in ministry. Therefore, they were called to enter into the Inner Court and minister before God's table and before His Ark. Their's was the privilege of offering the sacrifice's of fat and blood before God.

Zadok's company was to teach the people the difference between the holy and the profane – causing them to discern between the clean and the unclean. When there was a controversy, it was charged to stand in judgment, mandating God's laws and statues. Zadok's men would be separate and holy. God gave them instruction on how they should dress and how they should eat, and He provided them with promises of favor and blessing.

Zadok's sons are an example of a holy priesthood, an eternal standard for all to follow. This example illustrates our choice. We can decide to be priests that minister unto the Lord, or we can follow the path of compromise, trying to mix the holy with the profane, and become only doorkeepers.

Those priests who went astray and went their own way brought upon themselves eternal judgment and separation. Zadok's sons, who kept the laws and the commandments of the Lord when everyone else around them did not, were given a divine appointment to minister before the Lord and to offer sacrifices unto Him.

We have the same choice today. God cannot, and will not, tolerate or accept, anything that is not holy – separated unto Him. When we stand as His ministering priests, we do so in justice and holiness. When our lives are filled with mixture, the holy and the profane, it will be difficult for others to see if Christ lives within us or not. For those who choose to walk uprightly before Him, not wavering to compromise or to dilute their purity, a divine mandate awaits.

Seekers of His Face

There are two companies within God's ministers, two functioning priesthoods, just as there were in the days of the Levitical priesthood. The carnal priesthood operates with and thrives on compromise. Such priests are a sad blend of the godly and the worldly. They do not stand fast in their personal life, nor do they hold a firm hand to the House of the Lord. Their hearts are uncircumcised, and they entertain strangers in God's House, neglecting holy things. Their doctrines are based on compromise with man-made form and ritual. They steep themselves in tradition and have become motion without devotion, looking to please the masses by appearance, but not conforming to God's standards.

I do not mean to sound harsh, but I am calling upon the Church of the Lord Jesus Christ to take a stand. There is a dying, hungry and thirsty world looking to the Church for an example, and they cannot find it in our wine and cheese parties, aerobics classes, pageants, and "light" clubs. The call goes out for a priesthood made up of those whose lives are consecrated and whose hearts are repentant and circumcised.

Christ's Body will be whole and integral. He will not have any limb, any organ, any member, or part that isn't totally given to Him. We must be a company of priests whose lives have been dedicated to God and whose hearts are repentant and circumcised. We cannot be a body dripping with mixture.

Zadok stood faithful and holy in the midst of a perverse generation. He didn't bow to compromise, and his dedication was unaffected by the majority's call. To minister as Zadok's company, we must also stand guileless in His presence.

The Body of Christ is not anemic. It has His very life force flowing through it. In His blood there is salvation, deliverance, and healing. But His precious blood must not be offered to the world through unholy vessels.

CHAPTER FIVE

THE SHULAMITE AND THE DAUGHTERS OF JERUSALEM

T   *he song of songs, which is Solomon's. Let him kiss
      me with the kisses of his mouth: FOR THY LOVE
      IS BETTER THAN WINE.*

Song of Solomon 1:1-2

Solomon wrote a lyrical love song of longing and relationship. It is the story of a shepherdess and her beloved, and others who sought his love — the daughters of Jerusalem. A lifetime would not be sufficient to study all the types and shadows found in this song, for it is the Song of songs, the greatest of all songs.

In the song, there are three prominent figures: First, there is the Shulamite, a type of the Bride of Christ. Second, the Shepherd-King (two separate figures, though one person; both figures fulfill a place in the Shulamite's heart), a beautiful type of the Church's relationship with the Beloved, showing Jesus as each believer's Shepherd. He becomes our Shepherd when He becomes our Savior, the moment when our kinship with the Lord begins. The Christian learns to hear His comforting voice and to follow His leading, but He seeks to be not only Shepherd, but what is more important, King. His desire is to be Lord of every area of our lives.

Finally, there are the daughters of Jerusalem. They dwell within the city's gates, but they never venture out to know Him for themselves; this despite the King's love for them.

> *King Solomon made himself a chariot of the wood of Lebanon. He made the pillars thereof of silver, the bottom thereof of gold, the covering of it of purple, the midst thereof BEING PAVED WITH LOVE, FOR THE DAUGHTERS OF JERUSALEM. Go forth, O ye daughters of Zion, and behold king Solomon with the crown wherewith his mother crowned him in the day of his espousals, and in the day of the gladness of his heart.* Song of Solomon 3:9-11

It is immediately apparent that the daughters are quickly satisfied to be in His courts (at the gates), never longing for His chambers. However the Shulamite girl yearns for an intimate relationship with her Shepherd-King.

> *Draw me, we will run after thee: the king hath brought me into his chambers: we will be glad and rejoice in thee, WE WILL REMEMBER THY LOVE MORE THAN WINE: the upright love thee.* Song of Solomon 1:4

"Draw me," pleads the Shulamite, and the daughters of Jerusalem respond in chorus, *"We will run after thee."* In this one small verse we can find a hidden key to relationship. One seeker, the Shulamite, draws after herself many others. Her desire is contagious. All it takes is one person to start talking about food, and stomachs start to growl and mouths begin to water. Does our longing draw others in to respond? When you search after your Beloved, it can and will compel others to *"run after [Him]."*

The Shulamite and the Daughters of Jerusalem

The Shulamite is a seeker, longing for the chambers of her beloved. She says, *"Let him kiss me with the kisses of his mouth: for thy love is better than wine"* (Song of Solomon 1:2). Rapacious, avid desire, seeking a close individual relationship, is what she desires. Seeking is the key to relationship. When we seek Him we shall find Him Whom our heart desires.

Jerusalem's daughters also seek but, as we have already noted, they are too easily satisfied. They beg the Shulamite to return so they can look upon her and see the King:

> *Return, return, O Shulamite; return, return, that we may look upon thee. What will ye see in the Shulamite? As it were the company of two armies.* Song of Solomon 6:13

She must have worn His love well, for just looking upon her satisfied their desire.

What do people see when they look our way? Do they see something that causes them to *"taste and see that the Lord is good"* (Psalms 34:8)? Does our hunger cause others to seek? What picture do they see when they look our way? A believer's walk with God should compel others to enter a deeper relationship with Him. We should walk as seekers, compelling and provoking others around us to seek and know Him.

The Shulamite went on to say:

> *I rose up to open to my beloved; and my hands dropped with myrrh, and my fingers with sweet smelling myrrh, upon the handles of the lock. I opened to my beloved; but my beloved had withdrawn himself, and was gone: my soul failed when he spake: I sought him, but I could not find him; I called him, but he gave me no answer. The watchmen that went about the city found me, THEY SMOTE*

ME, THEY WOUNDED ME; THE KEEPERS OF THE
WALLS TOOK AWAY MY VEIL FROM ME. I charge
you, O daughters of Jerusalem, if ye find my beloved, that
ye tell him, that I am sick of love.

Song of Solomon 5:5-8

At the beginning of the song, the Shulamite and the
king fall in love, and the bride longs after her groom. Their
relationship is beautiful and they are united in love, but
then the Shulamite is faced with a struggle: she can't find
her beloved. Within the context of the song this dilemma
becomes something of a nightmare. As a shadow of the
relationship of the Church with the King, it is an illustration of genuine longing on the part of the Bride during
the Groom's absence.

Hearing her groom's voice, the Shulamite, goes to her
door, but briefly hesitates before rising to open it, something we will investigate more fully in another chapter. It
troubles her to find that he isn't there. She begins to seek
him with all her heart and strength. Running into the
streets, she calls after him.

She isn't familiar with the city. After all, she's only a
country girl. Then something deplorable happens. The
watchmen, who should have been on the wall, vigilantly
keeping and protecting the city, are about the streets. They
beat and wound her.

Chapter 3 of the Song presents the watchmen for the
first time. On that occasion, they simply seem ignorant
when the Shulamite asks them where her beloved has
gone. She looks a few steps beyond them and finds her
king. Obviously, the watchmen were failing to carry out
their job and calling.

Many times, when a watchman comes off the wall, his
place of calling, he is easily mired in the business of the

The Shulamite and the Daughters of Jerusalem

kingdom and loses sight of the king and His kingdom. When one leaves his place of responsibility, his priorities become confused. Perhaps these watchmen, removed from their posts, thought they were still seeking as they walked about the streets — looking in a new or unfamiliar place. However, if they had been at the station designated by their calling, above the narrow winding streets, they would have been able to see, and seeing, show others the way. They walked about, surely thinking they were seekers, but their purpose has been lost in the snarl of the city.

By chapter 5, the watchmen's apathy progresses to aggression, and they disgracefully beat the Shulamite. Not only have they ceased to seek the King, but they have become enemies of the Church. They find and beat the Shulamite, leaving her wounded.

These wayward men represent those who neglect their responsibility and their appointment. Their responsibility was to be on the wall, watching. Their appointment was to protect the city's people, not to inflict harm, but they have fallen from their high calling. They have lost their vision.

This is a sad and heartwrenching picture, but its gravity is worthy of note. The watchmen (pastors and ministers) who cease to seek their King (even though He is but a few steps away), not only ignore Him but fail to guide the Shulamite (the Church) to Him. However, the Shulamite, despite their incompetence, finds her Beloved.

These watchmen who first failed in their own search, and then in their responsibility to guide the Church, are soon found beating and wounding the very ones they had been commissioned to keep and protect. It is unfortunate, but there are many ministers who have become slack in seeking the King and have left the wall, and now, they only beat and wound their people, abusing them with a poor attitude and an empty ministry. Perhaps the marvelous thing is that the true believer, despite the failure of the watchmen, will find his or her King:

> *That they should seek the Lord, if haply they might feel after him, and find him, THOUGH HE BE NOT FAR FROM EVERY ONE OF US:* Acts 17:27

There is hope, even for wayward watchmen. If they will but turn and seek God with a repentant heart, they can again ascend to their positions on the city's wall and again proclaim a message worthy of their calling.

The Shulamite is beaten and wounded, and her veil (innocence) is torn from her, but even at that she can't be deterred from her search. She continues, sick with love for her King. The Church has been beaten and wounded, not only by enemies from within, but also by enemies from without. Millions of martyred believers have followed Stephen's example and wait under Heaven's altar (see Revelation 6:9-11).

The illustration of the Shulamite shows that being *Seekers of His Face* isn't easy. There is a price to be paid. Not every moment is spent in the King's inner chamber.

The Shulamite knows how cruel life's reality can be. She runs about in this present spiritual night looking for her Shepherd-King.

She has every reason for abandoning the search. What motivation could there be for her to continue to call out His name? There are enemies on all sides. Wouldn't it be easier for her to think, *He's too far away, too distant, set apart somewhere in His palace.* Her brief time with Him would seem to have been lost forever.

She might have viewed her own humble condition and

The Shulamite and the Daughters of Jerusalem

considered, *He's too good for me, I'm too lowly for the King.*
But she didn't. The beating didn't stop her, she did not
stop calling upon her Beloved. She couldn't and wouldn't
stop loving Him, even though He seemed so far away.
She sensed that He must be close.

The lesson that the Shulamite gives is: Don't let anyone, or anything keep you from seeking! So many Christians, when wounded by some situation in church or by
a minister, are quick to blame their spiritual indifference
on those who have done them harm and stop seeking.
The true believer, however, represented by the Shulamite,
keeps seeking, ignoring every power of evil that would
keep her from her intended goal!

The daughters of Jerusalem ask her:

> *Whither is thy beloved gone, O thou fairest among women?*
> *whither is thy beloved turned aside? that we may seek him*
> *with thee.* Song of Solomon 6:1

They say they want to join her in the search, but do
they really? Or are they mocking her? Perhaps some do
seek, but their journey is short-lived. They continually
find contentment where they are.

It is easy to see that the Shulamite has only one mo-
tive, only one purpose — she will find her King, and nothing will keep her from Him. Paul wrote:

> *Who shall separate us from the love of Christ? shall*
> *tribulation, or distress, or persecution, or famine, or na-*
> *kedness, or peril, or sword? As it is written, For thy sake*
> *we are killed all the day long; we are accounted as sheep for*
> *the slaughter. Nay, in all these things we are more than*
> *conquerors through him that loved us. For I am persuaded,*
> *that neither death, nor life, nor angels, nor principalities,*

nor powers, nor things present, nor things to come, Nor height, nor depth, nor any other creature, shall be able to separate us from the love of God, which is in Christ Jesus our Lord.   Romans 8:35-39

The Shulamite knows that her love can't be too far off. She tells the daughters of Jerusalem:

My beloved is gone down into his garden, to the beds of spices, to feed in the gardens, and to gather lilies. I AM MY BELOVED'S, AND MY BELOVED IS MINE: he feedeth among the lilies.   Song of Solomon 6:2-3

Christ, our Beloved, is never far away. This the true Bride knows. Though the night be long and dark, the Bride will soon find herself with her Groom — *among the lilies.* Seeking Him is where we begin and finding Him is where we receive. When we embrace Him, we are fulfilled. Let us become true *Seekers of His Face.*

CHAPTER SIX

TWO SISTERS: MARY AND MARTHA

N *ow it came to pass, as they went, that he en-*
tered into a certain village: and a certain woman
named Martha received him into her house. And
she had a sister called Mary, which also SAT AT JESUS'
FEET, and heard his word. But Martha was cumbered
about much serving, and came to him, and said, Lord, dost
thou not care that my sister hath left me to serve alone?
bid her therefore that she help me. And Jesus answered and
said unto her, Martha, Martha, thou art careful and trou-
bled about many things: But one thing is needful: and Mary
hath chosen that good part, which shall not be taken away
from her.   Luke 10:38-42

As we cross over into the New Testament, there are
examples of the two companies there as well. One such
example is found in the story of two sisters: Mary and
Martha. Many have seen Mary as the seeker and Martha
as the worker, but it's not as simple as that.

When Jesus entered the village where Mary and Martha lived, Martha, upon seeing Him, went out and invited
Him to her home. When He accepted her invitation and
entered their home, Mary sat at His feet listening to His
teachings, while Martha went back to work and busied
herself with *"much serving."* As a result, there have been
many negative commentaries about Martha. However,
Jesus Himself teaches us the importance of servanthood:

*BUT HE THAT IS GREATEST AMONG YOU SHALL
BE YOUR SERVANT. And whosoever shall exalt himself
shall be abased; and he that shall humble himself shall be
exalted.*   Matthew 23:11-12

Jesus could have made Martha a prime example of this important teaching.

Other New Testament passages also teach us the importance of being servants one to another (see Ephesians 6:6, Galatians 5:13, and Colossians 3:24). There must be more to the story of Mary and Martha than the issue of service.

Mary must have known how to serve as well. Martha, knowing this, spoke to Jesus concerning this issue. Mary specifically chose not to serve. The issue is not service. In fact, the issue is not clear until Jesus enters the house.

Martha was a seeker. After all, she was the one who went out to greet Jesus and invite Him to her home. Both sisters loved Jesus, and both welcomed His visit. It was only then, after Jesus was present in their home, that the difference between the two sisters becomes obvious.

Before He entered their home, the attitude of both sisters seemed the same. There was not noticeable difference in their opinions about the Master. Once Jesus was inside, however, the sisters took entirely different courses of action and their hearts' condition begin to show. Martha occupied herself in service and failed to realize Who had entered her home. Mary was immediately raptured above earthly care by the Lord's presence and found herself powerless to do anything but sit at His feet.

Martha's reaction to Jesus' presence is representative of the company that stands outside the inner court of worship, while Mary's response represents the inner-court company.

When Martha asked Jesus to tell Mary to help her, Jesus

looked beyond the situation and into Martha's need. He looked upon her heart. He saw many good intentions, but He required more. What He required wasn't for His benefit, but for Martha's. He was trying to help her. His concern was Her eternal portion.

Mary chose *the good part*. She chose first to worship and learn at the Master's feet. Jesus told her that what she had chosen had eternal value that could never be taken away from her.

Service isn't wrong, but when Jesus is present He demands our undivided attention. If our heart is centered on Him, then our service will show that we've been sitting at His feet. The lesson to be learned here is that true worship is true service.

As a minister, I must make a conscious effort to keep myself before the altar of the Lord. It is so easy to get busy, too busy. There is always so much to do that it become easy to lose sight of the genuine objective of worship – Jesus.

I must take time and sit myself down, without paper and pencil, and simply enjoy His Word, allowing it to pour into my spirit, falling in love with the One I find on every page. Failing to do this is dangerous to our spirits. Jesus gave a warning:

> *Many will say to me in that day, Lord, Lord, have we not prophesied in thy name? and in thy name have cast out devils? and in thy name done many wonderful works? And then will I profess unto them, I NEVER KNEW YOU: depart from me, ye that work iniquity.*   Matthew 7:22-23

Personally, I cry out to know Him. Paul wrote:

> *And be found in him, not having mine own righteousness, which is of the law, but that which is through the faith of*

Seekers of His Face

Christ, the righteousness which is of God by faith: THAT I MAY KNOW HIM, and the power of his resurrection, and the fellowship of his sufferings, being made conformable unto his death; If by any means I might attain unto the resurrection of the dead. Philippians 3:9-11

Such a declaration, coming from an apostle, might seem out of place. *"That I may know Him."* Didn't Paul know God? Obviously he did, so what is Paul trying to say?

Looking closely at the meaning of the word translated "knew" in this verse from Matthew and the word "know" from the verse in Philippians reveals a moving lesson. It is the same word that Hebrew custom uses to speak about the most intimate relationship between a man and his wife. So knowing Him is not a passing knowledge of His existence, but an intimate experience with Him.

When Jesus said that He *"never knew"* certain people, He meant that He never had an intimate relationship with them. They were too busy casting out devils and doing wonderful works to get to know Him intimately.

As ministers, we may study and search the Scriptures and preach a great message, but if we haven't entered the inner chambers with the Lover of our souls, we are only uninvited strangers in a place reserved for the most intimate relationship. Ministry begins and ends at Jesus' feet.

I love corporate worship, but long before I lift my hands to God in worship, I must lift my heart in surrender to Him. My own agenda must be laid aside. Only then can I bask in His presence. Then I am never worried about getting the hottest new revelation. I am never whispering my petitions into His ear. I simply look into His eyes that I may know Him.

The story of Martha and Mary doesn't end with this particular episode. Later, it is recorded that their brother Lazarus died, and the sisters were consumed with grief.

Two Sisters: Mary and Martha

In this account, Martha was again the first to meet Jesus. She was a seeker and had a degree of knowledge and revelation. She told Jesus that all He had to do was ask the Father to raise her brother, and He would do it. She had developed some level of relationship with the Lord. She had a mental knowledge, understanding that Jesus was who He said He was, and that God was His Father. She understood the power that came from the relationship between the Father and the Son. However, she didn't seem to demonstrate any true revelation of that knowledge.

As a seeker, she came to Him again, but she was interested in seeking Him for resurrection power, instead of seeking Him as the Resurrection.

Jesus saw past Martha's immediate need and circumstances and spoke to her heart: *"He that believeth in me, though he were dead, yet shall he live: And whosoever liveth and believeth in me shall never die. Believest thou this?"*

Was Jesus speaking about Lazarus? I don't think so. He was more concerned with helping Martha see, understand, and believe the eternal value of the moment. Jesus was speaking concerning Martha's heart. He knew that although she sought Him, she didn't yet have the relationship with Him that she needed.

When believers merely seek God for what He can do for them, their immediate circumstance or situation, may be resolved, but there won't be any eternal outcome. On the other hand, if we seek God for Who He is and we lay all our circumstances at His feet, not only will He deal with those circumstances, but there will be eternal benefits as well.

Like Martha, our personal revelation often begins with what we know. Martha knew that Jesus could heal her brother, but her confidence was in His arriving prior to Lazarus's death. Martha knew Jesus, but He was not yet a part of her.

Revelation begins with what we know, but it becomes a part of us, and part of our spirit in worship. The divine nature of Jesus is revealed and made life through relationship and worship. Martha would have known this if she had taken the time to worship at His feet when He entered the house. Instead, she was *"busy with much serving."*

The knowledge and revelation she did have was put to the test when Jesus commanded the stone to be rolled away. Martha, not knowing the divine nature of Jesus, responded, *"By this time he stinketh."* She did not know the resurrection nature of Jesus. She did not know nor believe the glory of God. Jesus asked her, "Said I not unto thee, that if thou wouldest believe, though shouldest see the glory of God?" Martha's revelation was limited. She had not yet fallen at the feet of the One she sought.

In this particular test, Mary didn't seem to do much better than Martha, although she had been at the Lord's feet. She simply wept as if she had no further hope. In fact, when Jesus saw her weeping with others of the Jews, John says that *He groaned in the spirit, and was troubled.*

Every believer is engaged in spiritual struggle. Mary, in this moment of weakness, was left hopeless, having no confession and only tears. Martha made a great confession, showing that she had matured in the things of God, but when it came time to test her confession, she found that she really hadn't come into everything that God had for her. Both sisters were still somewhat distant from God's perfect desire. But Jesus raised Lazarus from the dead despite their momentary failings!

A clear conclusion may be reached from this point. Relationship, KNOWING GOD, is more important in the long term than momentary triumphs and/or failures in a believer's experience. *"That we may know Him"* is the key to relationship.

CHAPTER SEVEN

TWO COMPANIES OF DISCIPLES

N ow as he walked by the sea of Galilee, he saw Simon and Andrew his brother casting a net into the sea: for they were fishers. And Jesus said unto them, COME YE AFTER ME, AND I WILL MAKE YOU TO BECOME FISHERS OF MEN. And straightway they forsook their nets, and followed him. And when he had gone a little further thence, he saw James the son of Zebedee, and John his brother, who also were in the ship mending their nets. And straightway he called them: and they left their father Zebedee in the ship with the hired servants, and went after him. Mark 1:16-20

Many people followed Jesus. Some of them mocked and rejected Him, while others were healed and delivered by His power. There were multitudes who sought Him, the seventy that He sent two-by-two to prepare for His coming to other places and, most particularly, there were twelve who fully devoted their lives to serving and following Him. They walked away from families, friends, and jobs, for His sake.

I've often pondered the lives of these men and the sacrifices they made to follow Jesus. When they were called, they didn't hesitate. Can such a level of commitment be found today? Are there people alive today who will follow Him, regardless of the cost to them of family, friends, or careers? Will there be those who choose that level of relationship and commitment?

Among the twelve disciples, those who became the twelve apostles, there were three in particular who had an intimate relationship with the Lord: Peter, James and John. They went with Jesus to the top of the mountain that has come to be called the Mount of Transfiguration, and something very unusual happened there:

And after six days Jesus taketh Peter, James, and John his brother, and bringeth them up into an high mountain apart, And was transfigured before them: and his face did shine as the sun, and his raiment was white as the light. And, behold, there appeared unto them Moses and Elias talking with him. Then answered Peter, and said unto Jesus, Lord, it is good for us to be here: if thou wilt, let us make here three tabernacles; one for thee, and one for Moses, and one for Elias. While he yet spake, behold, a bright cloud overshadowed them: and behold a voice out of the cloud, which said, THIS IS MY BELOVED SON, IN WHOM I AM WELL PLEASED; HEAR YE HIM. And when the disciples heard it, they fell on their face, and were sore afraid. And Jesus came and touched them, and said, Arise, and be not afraid. And when they had lifted up their eyes, they saw no man, save Jesus only. And as they came down from the mountain, Jesus charged them, saying, Tell the vision to no man, until the Son of man be risen again from the dead. Matthew 17:1-9

As these disciples watched, Jesus was transfigured or changed before their very eyes. They saw His face shine as brightly as the sun. His raiment turned as white as the light coming from Him, and they saw Elijah and Moses standing with Him.

Peter, seeing the three together, wanted to build three tabernacles. While he spoke concerning this, a cloud covered the mountain and God's voice was heard to say, *"This is my beloved Son, in whom I am well pleased; hear ye him."*

When the three disciples heard these words, they fell on their faces and were afraid. When they finally looked up, they saw only Jesus, and He commanded them not to tell anyone what they had seen until after His resurrection. It can be assumed that the three were trustworthy, or Jesus would never have given them the burden of keeping this secret.

The response of these three disciples to the transfiguration of Jesus showed worship (falling upon their faces) and relationship and a commitment (a desire to build three tabernacles). No one told them to worship, yet they fell upon their faces.

When a person has within his or her nature a desire to worship, no one needs to tell them to adore the Lord. At the mere sight of Him, those who worship Him in spirit and in truth will respond automatically and prostrate themselves in His presence.

Jesus knew these three men and knew their commitment to a covenant relationship with Him. Those who understand covenant hold fast no matter what circumstances may come their way.

When Jesus selected these three men to keep this astounding revelation a secret, He knew that this was no small thing. They had just witnessed one of the greatest revelations of all time and now must keep silent about it. And that had to be difficult. After all, once they had descended from the mountain's peak and were once again with the other disciples, there would be questions: "So what happened? What did you do? What did you see? What did He say?"

Though no doubt faced with such pressure, Peter, James, and John were faithful to Jesus' command in the coming days and months.

Of these three, there was a man named John. He was known as the disciple that Jesus loved. He, above all, enjoyed an intimate place by His Master's side:

> *Then Peter, turning about, seeth THE DISCIPLE WHOM JESUS LOVED following; which also leaned on his breast at supper, and said, Lord, which is he that betrayeth thee?*
> John 21:20

Does this mean that Jesus plays favorites? Certainly not. Jesus responded to John in a special way because John made the effort to press in to *KNOW* His Lord. He was the only disciple who laid his head on Jesus' bosom at the last supper. Reading the gospel that bears his name makes me doubt that he had the intention of being remembered for that particular moment. In fact, I doubt that John sought to be remembered at all.

With his every word, he was striving to reveal Jesus, for his desire was to know God and to please God. It was this desire that took John to the mountain, a place of great revelation and vision, a place where he would be obliged to live apart from the other apostles. His heart was not content with having seen God's manifestation, but his desire was also to reveal God to others. He wanted to see others walking in the same knowledge and relationship. In his first letter to the churches, he wrote:

> *That which we have seen and heard DECLARE WE UNTO YOU, that ye also may have fellowship with us: and truly*

Two Companies of Disciples

our fellowship is with the Father, and with his Son Jesus Christ. And these things write we unto you, that your joy may be full. This then is the message which we have heard of him, and declare unto you, that God is light, and in him is no darkness at all.   1 John 1:3-5

Clearly, the degree we seek God will determine to what degree we find Him, and the more we *know* Him, the more we will reveal Him to others. Jesus said:

Ask, and it shall be given you; seek, and ye shall find; knock, and it shall be opened unto you: For every one that asketh receiveth; and he that seeketh findeth; and to him that knocketh it shall be opened.   Matthew 7:7-8

Two companies. Two very different groups of people who, by reason of their own choice, seek and receive varying measures of blessing, or cursing, from God. Will you respond to Him in worship and obedience? Or will you be content to live on the outer fringes of His presence? God is looking for individuals who are willing to surrender all, to come and worship at His feet, laying aside everything else to worship Him *in spirit and in truth*. Those who choose to abide in His presence will partake of the divine nature and will ultimately be honored by becoming part of the *Lamb's Wife*.

PART II:

PREPARATION

CHAPTER EIGHT

A VESSEL CHOSEN

*N*ay but, O man, who art thou that repliest against
God? Shall the thing formed say to him that
formed it, Why hast thou made me thus? HATH
NOT THE POTTER POWER OVER THE CLAY, of the
same lump to make one vessel unto honour, and another
unto dishonour? What if God, willing to shew his wrath,
and to make his power known, endured with much
longsuffering the vessels of wrath fitted to destruction: And
that he might make known the riches of his glory on the
vessels of mercy, which he had afore prepared unto glory,
Even us, whom he hath called, not of the Jews only, but
also of the Gentiles?   Romans 9:20-24

In the Lord's house, Paul teaches, there are many different kinds of vessels. Some are *"of wrath,"* while others are *"of mercy."* Some are *"to honor,"* and some are *"to dishonour"*:

But in a great house there are not only vessels of gold and
of silver, but also of wood and of earth; and some to honour, and some to dishonour. If a man therefore purge himself from these, he shall be a vessel unto honour, sanctified,
and MEET FOR THE MASTER'S USE, AND PREPARED unto every good work.   2 Timothy 2:20-21

75

Some vessels endure for a long time, while others are easily broken and must be repaired or thrown away.

God is the potter, and we are His clay (see Isaiah 64:8). As the potter, He wants to form His people and mold them into vessels that are worthy of His name. This is our divine purpose in life (see Acts 9:15-16). For this to happen, however, God needs to find some pliable clay.

There is a specific place for every believer in the Body of Christ (see Romans 12:4-5). In the same way that many organs and limbs make up the human body, each believer has a specific place or function within the Body of Christ. The Father places each one person according to his or her particular grace (see Romans 12:6, Ephesians 4:8-12 and 2 Timothy 1:9-11). So, there are many vessels, each with a unique and special function, in the House of the Lord. Each one is uniquely made by the Lord Himself. He is the Master Potter:

> *The word which came to Jeremiah from the LORD, saying, Arise, and go down to the potter's house, and there I will cause thee to hear my words. Then I went down to the potter's house, and, behold, he wrought a work on the wheels. And the vessel that he made of clay was marred in the hand of the potter: So he made it again another vessel, as seemed good to the potter to make it. Then the word of the LORD came to me, saying, O house of Israel, CANNOT I DO WITH YOU AS THIS POTTER? saith the LORD. Behold, as the clay is in the potter's hand, so are ye in mine hand, O house of Israel. At what instant I shall speak concerning a nation, and concerning a kingdom, to pluck up, and to pull down, and to destroy it; If that nation, against whom I have pronounced, turn from their evil, I will repent of the evil that I thought to do unto them. And at what instant I shall speak concerning a nation, and con-*

A Vessel Chosen

cerning a kingdom, to build and to plant it; If it do evil in
my sight, that it obey not my voice, then I will repent of
the good, wherewith I said I would benefit them.

Jeremiah 18:1-10

One day God told his prophet Jeremiah to go down to the potter's house so that he could learn something important. A potter's work was an important part of every ancient community, and anyone who needed a certain vessel could find it there or, if not, have it especially made. There were vessels of all types to be found in the average potter's house. Some were for water, others for wine, and still others for many other uses. Some were considered to be more valuable than others in that they could hold treasures.

During my college days I had the opportunity of taking a pottery class as part of my major. I saw and experienced firsthand the relationship between the potter and the clay. The process is tedious, and the potter must take great care in each step if he or she is to make a beautiful vessel.

Before the work on the vessel begins, the potter selects a piece of clay – a very serious matter. There are many types of clay and to make a certain type of vessel the potter carefully chooses the type of clay he or she feels is right for the job. This is determined by the ultimate purpose of the vessel.

At the potter's house there is a clay pit. In that pit, there were several varieties of clay. The potter had to know his clay and choose not only the right type, but just the right lump, before beginning his work. Carefully he considered each lump, discerning its texture. In one, he might detect too much sand, and that would make the vessel too coarse for the purpose he envisioned. Some lumps would be knotty and hard, and if he applied pressure to them, they would pop open, revealing a crusty center.

Some of the lumps of clay had been on top too long and exposure to the elements, wind and air, had depleted their moisture. The potter would plunge them to the bottom of the pit, hiding them so that they might regain their useful qualities. He didn't stop searching until he felt he had found the perfect lump of clay for the job he was about to start.

Similarly, the Divine Potter tries the reins of our hearts, carefully looking into every chamber, inspecting it for sand, or for knots. Such imperfections as hurts, disappointments, and rejections will damage a lump. The list is long. When the Potter finds such blemishes, He carefully checks to see whether the lump is pliable in His hands. If it is, He can work out the impurities. If the lump is supple and responds to His touch, He takes it to His workroom. If not, He places it back in the pit until it is ready for fashioning.

After the potter has chosen the clay, he carefully washes it with clean water, and then he starts kneading it with firm hands. In this way, any foreign object, such as a stick or a rock, may be found and removed. If it is not removed, the extraneous item will become part of the finished work – spoiling it.

After he has washed and kneaded the clay, the potter puts it under his feet and treads on it to remove any air bubbles. If any air is left in the mix, the resulting vessels will pop or crack during the firing process and be ruined.

At each juncture, the potter feels the clay again, examining its condition. By simply touching it he knows exactly when it is ready and will be pliable, yielding to his hands on the wheel. And at each juncture, he applies more water to it, ensuring that the clay remains workable.

A Vessel Chosen

God's Word serves as the water that washes the lumps of clay that represents our lives. Paul wrote:

> *Husbands, love your wives, even as Christ also loved the church, and gave himself for it; That he might sanctify and cleanse it WITH THE WASHING OF WATER BY THE WORD, That he might present it to himself a glorious church, not having spot, or wrinkle, or any such thing; but that it should be holy and without blemish.*
>
> Ephesians 5:25-27

Constant washing with the water of the Word keeps Christians pliable in the hands of the Great Potter as He works to mold and form us into vessels of honor.

Never despise the kneading process. It is an important part of the preparation of the clay and, without it, a vessel worthy of honor simply cannot be developed. The minute you turn your life over to God, He begins to knead you. Then He treads on you. He is searching for all the sticks and stones that are stuck in you – all the hurts, the disappointments, the failures.

Expect any part of the lump that has not been carefully inspected and worked over by the Potter's hand to be inspected and worked over soon. If any part of the lump passes unwashed, improperly kneaded or trodden, it will be detrimental to the production of a quality product, and the failure of a small portion of the clay can result in the destruction of the whole. Impurities that remain hidden in the clay limit the Potter's effectiveness, so God must touch the believer's every thought, emotion, and memory.

The heat of the ovens often releases destructive forces. It is for this reason that much time is taken during the prepation period. The Father seeks those who will *act* according to His desire and not *react* according to their own agenda.

Several years ago I went through a series of hurts and disappointments. These experiences left me bruised, distrusting, and on the defensive. For months I withdrew from everyone. Convincing myself that I wasn't withdrawing, but that I was getting alone with God, I carried on, with "business as usual." I became careful about getting too close, or too personal, with other people, deciding that there was no need to interact with other people to be an effective minister. I thought, *I'll just love them, without receiving from them, and still be effective.* I was wrong.

One Sunday I walked into church, thinking that I had everything under control. I greeted everyone, smiled politely and engaged in courteous conversation. This went on until one of God's faithful servants came up and put her arms around me and didn't let go. I suddenly found myself sobbing in her arms. The dam had broken, and I wept uncontrollably.

I learned, from that, a lesson and discovered that turning things over to God is one thing, but that withdrawing is something else altogether. When we give God our hurts, it also means we give Him our trust. You cannot stay guarded or protective if you want to be healed. You must open up to Him, and that isn't always easy. Everything within us screams out for protection, and defensive walls go up faster than any mason could build them.

After that experience many people came up to me during the next several weeks and asked me what changed me so much. "Was it a conference you attended?" they asked.

In response, I simply smiled, and said, "I fell at the Great Potter's feet."

Jesus knows how to apply the tender strength of His

hands to perfect us. He only asks that we trust Him and remain pliable.

Jeremiah was to learn that God can even take a marred vessel and start over with it (see Jeremiah 18:4), as He had so many times with His people Israel. In His mercy, God makes provision for the backslider, the disobedient, the proud and the rebellious. If the heart is sincere, a person will find a place in the Potter's hand and upon His wheel. And it doesn't matter what our past has been, the skillful hands of the Potter can rework, refashion and reform us until He has smoothed away every imperfection.

King David must have understood this working of God better than most. The Psalms are full of David's thanksgiving to God for His faithfulness, forgiveness, and provision. David's heart cry was:

> *PURGE ME with hyssop, and I shall be clean: WASH ME, and I shall be whiter than snow. MAKE ME to hear joy and gladness; that the bones which thou hast broken may rejoice. CREATE IN ME a clean heart, O God; and RENEW a right spirit WITHIN ME.*   Psalm 51:7-8 and 10

If David were a member of many churches today, I'm afraid he might be cast aside, rejected, and scorned. It's sad to say, but he surely would not be accepted as a priest, prophet, or king. However, despite his weaknesses, the Lord still credited David with being *"a man after His own heart"* (1 Samuel 13:14 and Acts 13:22). David's willingness to be placed back on the wheel and reformed by the Potter's hand makes him an example to us all. In the end, he was indeed an honorable vessel.

After the potter, with powerful gentle hands kneads the clay, he is ready to place it on the wheel, otherwise known as the throwing wheel. The wheel moves continually in a circular motion and the clay is placed in the middle of the wheel on a plate. Using a kick plate the potter keeps that wheel spinning, for he never takes his hands off the mass. Constantly he forms it by adding water and by using the proper pressure. Spinning the vessel with steady tension ensures proper balance and weight.

With disciplined and careful hands, the potter makes meticulous adjustments at the proper times. If one side becomes too thin, he positions and maneuvers the clay, strengthening all sides proportionally. During his creative work, the potter is never a moment too soon or a second too late as he "throws" the clay.

There are certain moments in a believer's life when he or she feels the spinning and throwing that the Potter is using to form the vessel He desires. In the same manner that the kick bar keeps the wheel moving, life's circumstances keep the believer spinning. To maintain pliability, the Master Potter uses the perfect combination of water and pressure. When there is resistance, He adds just the right amount of pressure in the right place, until the forming vessel renders itself to His gentle, but powerful, touch. And if the believer's clay is still too tough or impure, it is His delight to stop the process and start all over again. He knows that by refusing to pass on a defective vessel, He can form an even better one (see Hosea 6:1).

Having been given a final form, the vessel is ready for the next step, the drying (or waiting) process. This is a painful process for the believer. You have been called out of the pit, prepared, formed, and fashioned, and there you sit, a ready vessel ... or are you? If a vessel is not allowed to sit and dry, all the properties that have been worked into its design will not stand up in the firing.

It is in the firing process that the vessel experiences extreme temperatures. It is here that the qualities the potter sought during the preparation period will emerge. When a vessel is brought from the furnace, it will have ceramic qualities. It will be solid, concrete, firm, and fixed. It will be a beautiful creation.

A true vessel is formed by constant pressure and is made useful by intense heat. A vessel that cannot withstand drying and firing renders itself of little value and use.

When the Heavenly Potter allows us to go through the fires, it is not just so that He can watch us sweat. He knows that the fire is hot, but He also knows that we can endure it, that it will last for a short season and that we will be perfected by it. When the time of fiery trials has done its work, the vessel will emerge, fit for the Master's use. Slighting or avoiding any part of the process — whether throwing, drying, or baking — will cause the vessel to collapse under the pressure of use.

One day, when I was about seventeen, I heard the Spirit of the Lord say to me, "I'm going to give you a rod of iron in your back."

I remember thinking, *"Yeah ... great. Thank You."*

I had no idea what God was really saying. In my mind, I had a picture of God opening up my back and sovereignly placing a rod of iron in it. I thought that this word meant that He was going to give me strength to endure any situation. But several weeks went by and the bottom seemed to drop out of my life. I began to experience all manner of difficulty. I began to realize that the intense heat of life's circumstances would form, hammer, and strengthen the rod God had promised to place in me.

I wish I could say that it happened overnight, but the process took several years and required some heartbreaking circumstances. Looking back, it has not been a trek that I would eagerly repeat, nonetheless, I'm eternally grateful for God's workmanship in me.

There is one final aspect of forming a vessel that I wish to cover. It involves those vessels that have been fashioned, dried, and fired and are now active in their God-given function. Vessels, because of use, are often in need of repair. With time they become structurally weakened. Perhaps they have been dropped or handled roughly and they need a fresh touch from the potter's hand. Every believer eventually reaches this condition. So when repair time comes, learn to recognize it and don't resist what God is doing in your life.

A vessel in need of repair can show its lack in several ways. Its mouth can become worn from constant use and its ability to pour is impaired. Its interior can be damaged if it isn't properly and regularly emptied. Without faithful and thorough washing, it is in danger of becoming hard and crusty with old residue. When this happens, the residue will effect the contents of the vessel and using it becomes a chore, rather than a joy.

Such a vessel should be taken to the potter's house for refashioning. There, the potter can empty, scrape, sand and polish the vessel, using the proper tools. At the potter's house, the vessel first experiences the process of being emptied. Believers must occasionally be emptied of everything so that the Master can refill them with something fresh and new. And, for a believer, this isn't an easy thing. It is contrary to a vessel's nature to be left empty. So to make it through this difficult time, one must rely on God's promises.

When the Potter pours everything out of you, everything you have fought for, worked for, waited for, or sought after comes out, and everything you are must fall at His feet. This is a process from which no believer is

A Vessel Chosen

exempt (see 2 Corinthians 3:18). Each time God changes me, taking me from glory to glory, He first empties me and dries me out. This can be a terrifying process.

Fruit-bearing plants are the result of the death of a seed (see John 12:24). We must each die before we can bring forth fruit. In order for me to walk in the fullness of God's character, He must first leave me empty of self:

> *Always bearing about in the body the dying of the Lord Jesus, that the life also of Jesus MIGHT BE MADE MANI-FEST IN OUR BODY. For we which live are alway deliv-ered unto death for Jesus' sake, that the life also of Jesus might be made manifest in our mortal flesh.*
> 2 Corinthians 4:10-11

After the potter empties a vessel, he meticulously scrapes out all the residue that has built up in it. Often, a person will want to hold on to his hurts and disappoint-ments, just as he holds on to his achievements. Pain and hurt become a familiar and faithful friend. They can be-come a part of a person's life and character, but to be-come a vessel of honor, such hurt and rejection will have to be poured out, leaving nothing for self. Once that old residue is gone, the Potter replaces it with sweet victory, joy, and peace.

Vessels that have been mishandled, abused, dropped, cracked, or chipped, especially over a long period, need to be smoothed. Otherwise, broken and rough edges may snag and scratch those who work with that vessel. To re-store it, the potter sands and scraps the broken edges un-til all signs of abuse are gone.

A vessel's owner must have great confidence and trust when he turns it over to a potter. If the potter's hand were to slip, it could devastate the vessel and render it useless.

When the Potter is the Lord, we can have absolute trust. He is careful to sand one area at a time.

After the vessel has gone through each process, the potter may need to add new clay in areas where the vessel has worn thin. Finally, he refires it, and all the valuable properties that the vessel once had are now restored.

The most painful part of this entire procedure, perhaps, is not being emptied or scraped, but the inactivity the vessel must endure in the process. If a vessel patiently endures the entire process he or she will emerge with fresh splendor and every moment of the long wait will have been worth it.

Of the many vessels at the potter's house, one occasionally emerges from the fire with significant beauty. The fire has brought out some quality that the others don't have. When this happens, the potter takes it aside and reserves it for a specific time and place.

One day I was studying the story of the potter's house and the Lord gave me an insight into the relationship between the Bride and the Potter. I saw the potter's house and a certain man entering. He asked the potter for a vessel that he could take to a wedding. There were many vessels on the shelves, and the potter showed him one after another. The man carefully looked at each one, turning it over and over, examining every detail. He continued looking around until asking, "Is there a vessel that I can take to a wedding?"

Turning, the potter looked deep into the man's eyes and then exited into a smaller room in the back of his house. When he emerged, in his hands he carried a vessel, shiningly flawlessly. Its beauty was unmistakable.

The potter carefully gave the vessel to the man, who received it in like manner. He examined every detail, until finally he turned it upside down. A moment later he smiled with great delight and turned to the potter, who had been watching quietly. He said, "This vessel has been touched by the Master's hand, and it bears His name."

Only those vessels that carry the Master Potter's mark will be found worthy to enter the Marriage Supper of the Lamb. To make them, the Lord is looking for pliable clay, ready to be molded by His hands. He wants to make vessels of endurance, those that can survive every part of the long process and endure the fires of affirmation. From it, a distinguished and beautiful vessel will emerge, and He will be proud to seal such a vessel with His name.

CHAPTER NINE

FAVOUR OBTAINED

*L et us be glad and rejoice, and give honour to him:
for the marriage of the Lamb is come, and HIS WIFE
HATH MADE HERSELF READY.*

Revelation 19:7

There is a call emanating from the throne of God compelling us to draw near. There is a choice to be made. We can choose to remain where we are, we can draw back, fleeing from the call, or we can choose to draw near. Those who choose to draw near choose to embrace a process of preparation which will lead to the marriage of the Lamb. All will gather, but those who have made themselves ready, choosing to embrace the drawing of the Spirit of God, will have the honor of being called *"the Lamb's wife."*

To better understand the picture of the Bride we will look at the life of Esther. Hidden in her life is the preparation of the Bride. Esther was a young maiden who obtained favor in the eyes of the king. As a result, she was granted the honor of becoming his queen.

The book bearing Esther's name is a rather short historical account of a short historical period, but its importance goes much further.

Just as Abraham sent his servant to find a bride for his son Isaac (see Genesis 24:3), the Holy Spirit is preparing a spotless Bride for God's Son. We can learn from Esther how to become part of that Bride.

Several important individuals emerge in the book:

Queen Vashti represents the spirit of man that refuses to draw near at the King's request.

Esther represents the born-again heart, yielded and committed to the house of preparation. She allowed Mordecai, her cousin, to direct and lead her in all things. Mordecai, therefore, represents the Holy Spirit. He never left her gates and never compromised.

King Ahasuerus may represent several things but, for the sake of this study, he is a figure of the Heavenly Bridegroom.

Esther and Mordecai had an enemy that sought to destroy them and their people. He was the wicked Haman and represents the flesh, which seeks to sit upon the throne of our lives and to overcome the spirit:

> *Now it came to pass in the days of Ahasuerus, (this is Ahasuerus which reigned, from India even unto Ethiopia, over an hundred and seven and twenty provinces:) That in those days, when the king Ahasuerus sat on the throne of his kingdom, which was in Shushan the palace, In the third year of his reign, he made a feast unto all his princes and his servants; the power of Persia and Media, the nobles and princes of the provinces, being before him: When he shewed the riches of his glorious kingdom and the honour of his excellent majesty many days, even an hundred and fourscore days.* Esther 1:1-4

King Ahasuerus was over a vast empire, stretching from India to Ethiopia. It included a hundred and twenty-seven provinces or states. After he had reigned for three years Ahasuerus decided to make a great feast for all the princes, nobles, and servants who lived in his province. He wanted to show the people his great wealth, his power, and the glory of his kingdom. It was indeed magnificent.

In the garden court of the king's palace, upon the wall were hangings of white, green, and blue. They were fastened to silver rings on marble pillars with cords of white linen and purple. The floor was made of red, black, blue, and white marble. But everywhere the guests wandered within the king's palace during the one-hundred-and-eighty-day event, they could see his wealth and power exhibited.

During the final days of the feast the king invited all those in Shushan, both great and small to dine with him. Each received a vessel of fine gold from which to drink the king's wine. Each cup was unique. Contrary to custom, which would have demanded that all drink the same amount together, the king ordered that each guest could drink as much, or as little, of the king's wine as they wished.

As a figure, this points to the believers' invitation to drink from God's cup of fellowship. Each one chooses to drink as much or as little as he will. The Heavenly King never forces the cup of fellowship and communion upon anyone, but offers it freely.

As the feast reached its climax, the king called for his queen, desiring to show his guests what he considered to be his greatest possession. She was a indeed a very beautiful woman. But when one of the chamberlains went to bid Vashti to come, she refused.

King Ahasuerus was understandably angry and asked his advisors what he should do about the queen's insubordination. What would happen if all the rest of the women in the kingdom followed her example?

The counselors agreed and advised the king to banish

Vashti and replace her with some other fair maiden. This advice was accepted, Vashti was banished from the kingdom and all the subjects of Shushan were duly advised.

For those who would live in God's Kingdom, the rebellious, unyielding soul must be banished — all willful thoughts cast aside — and the choice made to draw near at the King's invitation.

Among the fair maidens of King Ahasuerus' realm was Esther. She lived with her cousin Mordecai, who had taken her when her parents died and had raised her as his own daughter:

> *Now in Shushan the palace there was a certain Jew, whose name was Mordecai. ... And he brought up Hadassah, that is, Esther, his uncle's daughter: for she had neither father nor mother, and THE MAID WAS FAIR AND BEAUTI-FUL; whom Mordecai, when her father and mother were dead, took for his own daughter.* Esther 2:5-7

Esther had begun preparing herself for greatness early in life. Living in the house of Mordecai, a type of the Holy Spirit, she had been embraced by him as his own. It was his care that fashioned her life and character.

In the same way, each one that enters the King's courts must be first prepared by the ministry of the Holy Spirit.

No sooner had Mordecai brought Esther and presented her to Hegai, at the king's house of preparation, than she found favor in his eyes, and he quickly gave her all the things she needed for her purification. Esther was to spend the next twelve months in that house, a ministry that may be likened to that of the Church:

> *And he gave some, apostles; and some, prophets; and some, evangelists; and some, pastors and teachers; FOR THE*

Favour Obtained

PERFECTING OF THE SAINTS, for the work of the ministry, for the edifying of the body of Christ:

Ephesians 4:11-12

When God's delegated authority flows properly through His established ministers towards His people, and the people allow that authority to flow within their lives, they are perfected, equipped, and prepared for the work of the ministry. They will ultimately rule and reign with Christ.

For too long I have heard people speaking in a negative manner concerning this principle of leadership established by God Himself for the Church. They often substitute the word "control" for the word "perfection." Perhaps this happens because the authority they have been under abused or misused his or her authority and the result for them has been control, not perfecting or equipping. But this is certainly not God's intent. I'm afraid that when many people refer to others trying to "control" them it is because they still have a rebellious heart.

There is still a lack of teaching in the Body of Christ on the purpose of the ministries God has placed in the Church, and without proper teaching concerning the place of these ministries, many do not know how to respond when faced with a pastor's instruction or correction.

There are five specific and unique ministry gifts which God brings to His people through individuals that He has commissioned. Such commissioned ministers have delegated authority from God for perfecting His people. It can be a painful process for both the pastored and the pastors.

The pastor's work is much like a parent. Each parent has the responsibility of seeing to it that the lives God has entrusted to his or her care reach their full potential.

Those children must be groomed with loving guidance, correction, and instruction. The ultimate goal is to present to society a mature, equipped, and responsible adult.

As any parent can tell you, it is not always a popular job. Parents must make tough decisions, establishing unpleasant guidelines and restrictions. They understand that it's all in their children's best interest, even when the children accuse their parents of "controlling" their lives. It does hurt when a parent hears these harsh accusations from a child's mouth, but because parents know that what they are doing is for the child's best interest, they must continue to train, correct, and instruct.

When people come to me using the word "control" too harshly and accuse a delegated authority in the church, I look first at the life and heart bringing the charge. I generally ask the person to tell me what he or she believes the word control means. Frequently, upon hearing the perception and definition, it isn't difficult to assess that the problem isn't the pastor, but rather, the individual who brought the charge. Cases such as this are similar to those in which children have problems with their parent's guidelines.

I know this isn't a well-liked subject, but I believe it's time to embrace the ministry within the Church, where God, according to His will, has placed us. His purpose is to bring us into perfection. Christians expect that the only words they will hear from their ministers will be gracious, but I believe we have had enough sympathetic counsel and pats to last a lifetime. It's grow up time for the Church. Christ's purpose with His Church is to bring it to perfection. This is work, and He has chosen to use delegated authority through His ministers to get it done. He cannot use individuals who will not embrace correction, instruction and grooming by His chosen ministers.

Favour Obtained

It is an error and the result of deception when believers refuse the Lord's outstretched hand through God's own ministers. It is erroneous to believe, or even to think, that one is exempt from instruction by His appointed servants. Refusal of God's delegated authority is refusal of the Holy Spirit Who has empowered the ministerial operation for the Church.

However, when God's ministers attempt to operate outside of their authority, it is God's responsibility to harness them, not ours. Remaining teachable is our only responsibility.

In Hegai's house, Esther was to be prepared for the king, and ultimately, for ruling and reigning. There were two elements in Esther's preparation: patience – waiting for the passage of time – and purification. In obedience, she moved in these two elements and, as a result, she obtained great favor.

All too often, some individuals hear a word from the Lord and take off like a racehorse out of the gate, without first being properly prepared, not yet having endured patiently through the test of time and the purification. By passing through a period of preparation we learn obedience. Isaiah said:

And he hath made my mouth like a sharp sword; in the shadow of his hand hath he hid me, and made me a polished shaft; in his quiver hath he hid me;　　Isaiah 49:2

To make a polished shaft there are several things that a branch must go through. First the craftsman selects a particular branch from a tree. Secondly, he plucks all the leaves from it, removing its beautiful foliage and leaving only a bare branch. Perhaps the leaves were beautiful and pleasant to the eye, but they cover the useful material that lies beneath.

Now that the craftsman has removed the leaves, all that remains is the bare, crooked, knotty branch, but the skilled archer looks beyond the knots and crooks to see its potential. The branch doesn't automatically become a polished shaft when picked from the tree.

The third step is the straightening of the branch. A craftsman doesn't have to look for a straight branch. He knows that he can straighten most any branch, but only if it will bend. To begin the bending, he soaks the branch in water for days. Water is locked into the branch's fibers, making it pliable. If the fibers don't absorb the water, then the branch snaps in the press.

The fourth step is the press. Now saturated with water, the craftsman places the branch in a press, or grip, and allows it to dry under pressure, forcing it to straighten.

Fifthly, the craftsman removes the shaft from the press and rubs it with oil so that its fibers won't turn brittle. After thoroughly rubbing it with oil, he gives the branch a tip and suddenly it is no longer a branch, but an arrow.

The tip he applies has been hammered out ahead of time and has been weighted for the shaft. It has been waiting for placement at the proper time. Piercing the air, the tip will open the way for the shaft to travel through the air, deliberately and accurately, enabling it to hit its intended mark.

Isaiah spoke of the "*quiver*" into which the shaft is placed. After the shaft has gone through the preparation process and has received its tip, it is then placed in a quiver until the time it is needed. It is the hardest process the shaft must pass through. It has been picked, stripped, soaked, anointed, and given a tip, and it is ready to do some serious work for God. But now it must wait in the quiver – hidden in the shadow of His hand – until the appointed time.

The season of waiting, hidden in God's quiver, can be frustrating, lonely, and often discouraging. But if we trust Him and let the season run its course, great rewards await us.

The quiver experience is humbling. It will work the "I" out of "glorified." It takes the quiver experience to bring out character – God's character.

When the time comes, the Lord removes the polished shaft that He has guarded so carefully, and He shoots it forth. When released, it will hit the mark for which it was designed.

Esther was willing to patiently submit herself to preparation, regardless of how long it took. Hegai, whose name means *meditation,* maintained the house of preparation.

When we are in God's quiver, when we are in His house of preparation, there is time to think, to meditate, to reflect on Him. Meditation in God's presence brings a clear perspective and a clear vision. In such meditation, eyes become fixed, and ears become acutely tuned. It is part of the process necessary to prepare one to enter into the King's court.

Those who refuse to bow their knees in the house of preparation will never be privileged to bow in the King's presence. The house of preparation teaches obedience and submission.

During the first six months of Esther's stay in the house of Hegai, she was anointed with myrrh – an oily extract from a bush used as an ointment for healing. Myrrh is most fragrant when dripped or rubbed, but when its oil hardens, what was fragrant to smell becomes bitter to taste. Myrrh represents God's dealings with us, breakings, and testings, that He sends our way. God's dealings with us can be pleasant, but if we refuse or resist, it can become disagreeable.

Myrrh is also a type of death. True life comes only through death. Jesus, soon after His birth, was presented with a gift of myrrh. This was a reminder that He, as no other, was born to die for the redemption of the lost.

Myrrh was also found at the cross. In Christ's birth we are reminded of His death, and in His death, we are reminded of His resurrection life.

Myrrh is the fragrance that comes from brokenness. After being broken, the believer is ready to be anointed with *"sweet odors and spices"* from the house of preparation. Esther, in submitting to the required processes in the house of preparation, allowed herself to be broken. As a result she was made beautiful, a bouquet of desire, and soon she was ready to be presented to the king.

Custom granted that each maiden could carry with her anything that might catch the king's eye on the day when, having finished her preparation, she was brought before the king (see Esther 2:13 and 15). Esther chose to enter, presenting nothing but herself. Her time in Mordecai's care had won her favor in the eyes of Hegai. A work of beauty and of grace had been done in her and it was visible to others. In Hegai's house, she had deepened her preparation with the anointing from myrrh and spices. Apparently, Hegai, seeing Esther's beauty, counseled her not to take anything else. She could go before the king with nothing in hand.

When we are called before the throne, our King prefers to see us with nothing in our hands. He doesn't want to see our achievements, our talents, or our gifts. He is looking only to see if we have been to the house of preparation, if we have been perfumed, if we bear the beauty

Favour Obtained

of God's preparations in the Spirit. When we emerge, there will be a visible beauty that all may see. But we are not being prepared for others. We are being prepared for the King's pleasure, and it is Him we desire to please.

When Esther was taken before the king and he looked upon her, she *"obtained grace and favor ... more than all of the virgins."* Without any fanfare, the king placed the royal crown upon her head.

A call resounds from God's throne for believers to draw near. Those who choose to obey will first be taken to the house of preparation. There they will be anointed with myrrh, broken, and tested. In brokenness they will be anointed with sweet odors and spices. And when they come before the King, He will look into their eyes and see a reflection of Himself.

The Scriptures mention one other account of Esther receiving favor in the presence of the king. During her stay in the king's palace, Esther's faithful uncle never left the gate. He knew that Esther was in the palace for a divine appointment and so he waited day and night, carefully monitoring those who entered:

> *And when the virgins were gathered together the second time, then Mordecai sat in the king's gate. Esther had not yet shewed her kindred nor her people; as Mordecai had charged her: for Esther did the commandment of Mordecai, LIKE AS WHEN SHE WAS BROUGHT UP WITH HIM.*
> Esther 2:19-20

Haman had been promoted to the king's right hand, but his motives were evil and his eyes were on the throne (see Esther 3:1-6). He sought power, authority, and honor. He persuaded the king to make a decree stating that all the servants who sat in the king's gate were to bow when he passed. Mordecai was among those servants.

The day came that Haman passed through the gate and everyone bowed except Mordecai. He refused to bow or reverence anyone but the king. As an example of the Holy Spirit, he refused to bow to flesh. Flesh wages a daily war to be on the throne, but the Holy Spirit stands watching day and night, guarding the gate to the believer's life. He upholds God's standards and will not bow to flesh, will not reverence man, will not compromise.

We are constantly bombarded by the desires of the flesh. Sights, sounds, tastes, and feelings easily motivate one's eyes, ears, and mouth, which are the gates to the heart. Not only is passage to the heart through these gates, but also passage from the heart. This means that what is in the heart will be reflected on the outside through these gates. Others will see, hear, and feel what is abundant in the heart of the Christian.

Each day that Haman passed Mordecai refused to bow. This created such anger in Haman that he sought a way to destroy Mordecai and all the Jews with him.

Hearing of Haman's evil plan, Mordecai rent his clothes, and dressed in sackcloth, covering himself in ashes.

Esther's maids heard that Mordecai was mourning and sent word to her. She began to grieve and sent Mordecai clothes to take away his shame, but he would not accept them.

The Holy Spirit is a person and not a thing and, as a person, He feels emotion. Believers who disobey and compromise, by bowing to anyone other than King Jesus, grieve the Holy Spirit. Once grieved, nothing can disguise or cover up His grieving. It will not just go away just because we want it to. The Holy Spirit never compromises

Favour Obtained

His grief just because it makes us feel uncomfortable or it forces us to deal with the situation that has caused His grief.

Esther, hearing Mordecai's report, wanted to see the king promptly. But to save Esther from danger and possible death, Mordecai, upon hearing of her intention, sent word for her to hold her peace. Esther respected Mordecai's wisdom and took time to pray and fast for three days.

As prayer and fasting was essential for Esther, so too prayer and fasting is essential for those who want to enter into the Heavenly King's throne room. Prayer and fasting prepares hearts. It is not intended to help God, but to help the believer. Those who pray and fast bring their will under subjection to His. They crucify their own agenda and prepare themselves to appear before Him.

Having fasted and prayed, Esther was ready to enter the king's presence. To do so without an invitation, however, could mean certain death (see Esther 4:10-12).

Esther decided to dressed herself in her royal robes. The Scriptures declare:

> *But ye are a chosen generation, a ROYAL priesthood, an holy nation, a peculiar people; that YE SHOULD SHEW FORTH THE PRAISES of him who hath called you out of darkness into his marvellous light:*   1 Peter 2:9

When we go before the King, how do we present ourselves? Do we wear the garments of praise or the garments of heaviness?

Esther knew that her life would be in the balance (see Esther 5:1-2), but after three days she entered the king's court, prepared for whatever might happen. Once there, she waited for him to notice her. It was part of the law that no one could enter in before the king without being called. You would think, however, that the queen would be the exception. Esther's example shows that none can enter the celestial throne room, or approach God, based on their own worthiness or righteousness. And there are no exceptions.

As partakers of the New Covenant, today's believers do not live according to the Law. God has torn the veil, giving free access to Heaven's throne room. Still, those who enter would do well to learn the valuable lesson of waiting before the King.

Those who seek to enter sometimes forget that they serve a holy and righteous King and they rush forward without grace. This is an abuse of our open and free access to God's presence, yet it is a reflection of the culture that surrounds the Church today. Has democracy taken away all our respect for royalty?

Perhaps it is because we have been so freely given access into the throne room, or perhaps it is because we do not live in a country that has a reigning monarch, that we are not aware of the respect given to royalty. The way to the throne is now available but it is not free. It is paved with costly and precious sacrifice, the blood of our dear Savior. The King of kings who sits upon the throne is worthy of both honor and glory. He deserves proper worship and proper approach. The next time we want to appear before God, before rushing in, we would do well to wait for His outstretched hand. Yes, the way to the throne is open to all, but there is a price to be paid. Esther was prepared to pay with her life if that became necessary. She was courageous and bold, but she knew how to find mercy and grace by waiting patiently.

Jesus has made a path to the throne with His costly

and precious blood. The King of kings, upon His throne, is worthy of honor and glory. He deserves proper worship and proper approach. We are taught:

Let us therefore come boldly unto the throne of grace, that we MAY OBTAIN MERCY, and find grace to help in time of need.   Hebrews 4:16

Isn't Esther a beautiful model for entrance into the King's inner court? She came with proper preparation, clothed with royal robes, she entered boldly but waited for grace.

Esther's preparation in fasting, her patience to wait, led to her favor. When the king saw her, he held out his scepter with his right hand and extended it to her. By this act, he granted her entrance into the inner court. She drew close and touched his scepter. She had obtained favor with the king. She had been willing to pay the ultimate price, but instead she had received grace.

Frequently one struggles to hold on to self, but finally, when self is placed on the altar of sacrifice, like Abraham's sacrifice of Isaac, the promise is restored, grace and favor are added.

There are times when we must enter the King's court, just as we are, yet He opens His arms and graciously welcomes us. There are other times when the Holy Spirit speaks and says, "Hold thy peace." He is calling for proper preparation and royal attire. Lay self on the altar, wait for Him to call you near, and divine favor will come, just as it did to Esther.

I believe that there is a portion of divine anointing and authority that the Church has yet to receive because she has so often rushed into the King's court. Patient waiting isn't easy. Esther's brief moment of tarrying before the king must have seemed dreadfully long to her. But in waiting she obtained favor and authority, the outstretched scepter of the king.

The life of Esther is an illustration for Christ's Bride, the Church. Her preparation, her trials, and her victory brought her the royal crown and salvation for her people. As Esther allowed herself to be prepared and tested, the Church must also, and the result will be favor obtained.

CHAPTER TEN

FIXED EYES

*B*EHOLD, THOU ART FAIR, MY LOVE; *behold,*
thou art fair; thou hast doves' eyes within thy locks:
thy hair is as a flock of goats, that appear from
mount Gilead. Song of Solomon 4:1

As we have seen, Solomon's Song bears a timely message. Some Christians cry to the Lord for blessing or
comfort. Others long for healing or provision. But our
greatest cry should be to know Him. If you have found
yourself crying out, "Father, I want to know You more,"
then you are being drawn to Him.

The Song of Solomon is a beautiful image of hunger,
desire, and fulfillment. It describes relationship and the
key to intimacy with the Beloved. In its pages, we don't
have to look far to find ourselves and our own search for
intimacy with the King.

We've already been introduced to the Shulamite and
the other personalities found in the Song. We have also
seen the depth of her relationship with the Beloved and
noted that she represents the Bride of Christ. In this symbolic capacity, she guides the way to affinity with the

Shepherd-King and takes us on a journey that increases our knowledge and our revelation of the Lord.

If we choose to listen closely to the Song, God's message, coming from His throne, will draw us and prepare us to sing the Lamb's song.

In the Song of Solomon, there are many shadows and representations, and there are many ways to look at them. It is a book that must be interpreted prophetically and not literally. It is written in everyday language but is filled with words of love and longing.

Earlier we identified the Beloved as King Jesus. There may be other possible interpretations, and each has its own merits, but we have chosen this one because it so wonderfully describes our King, our Beloved.

Also, as noted, the Shulamite is a figure of the Church, who seeks to know the Beloved. She desires an intimate relationship with her Beloved. No casual relationship will do. She wants the relationship of intimacy, the relationship of the Bride, the inner chamber. And the Beloved seeks the same.

The Bride's cry isn't a flippant one — not mere words that she says without thinking. Instead, she expresses longing and her Lover (Christ) consumes her every thought. "Draw me, we will run after thee." How many time have we cried, "Draw me," and when He does, we don't respond? All of our good intentions mean nothing unless we follow them with an expression of obedience.

Perhaps she once sought Him for what He offered, but now she wants more. She isn't looking at what He does, but at Who He is.

During the course of the Song, the Shulamite dines at her Beloved's banqueting table, is anointed with sweet fragrances, and then is carried in His chariot through the wilderness. In everything, she is consumed with her love:

Fixed Eyes

I sleep, but my heart waketh: it is the voice of my beloved
that knocketh, saying, OPEN TO ME, my sister, my love,
my dove, my undefiled: for my head is filled with dew, and
my locks with the drops of the night.

Song of Solomon 5:2

Notice how the Beloved knocked at her door: not with his fist, but with His voice, calling to her. This was the accepted way of "knocking" on a door in Middle Eastern culture.

Jesus stands at our door, knocking, gently calling. He won't beat on the door with His fist, but He calls to us, compelling us to answer His invitation and let Him in (see Revelation 3:20).

Of the Shulamite, it was said, her *"heart waketh."* She has expectation and desire, but she has already taken off her coat, washed her feet, and nestled down for the evening, when suddenly there is a knock at her door:

I have put off my coat; how shall I put it on? I have washed
my feet; how shall I defile them? My beloved put in his
hand by the hole of the door, and my bowels were moved
for him. I rose up to open to my beloved; and my hands
dropped with myrrh, and my fingers with sweet smelling
myrrh, upon the handles of the lock. I opened to my be-
loved; but my beloved had withdrawn himself, and was
gone: my soul failed when he spake: I sought him, BUT I
COULD NOT FIND HIM; I called him, but he gave me
no answer.   Song of Solomon 5:3-6

We looked at the Shulamite's determination to find her Beloved, and the suffering she went through to do it, but isn't it curious that she just missed Him? As they say, "So near, and yet so far away." A moment's hesitation cost her dearly. Yes, her heart was awake, and yes, she hadn't lost her desire, but she was indisposed.

Love is often tested at the most inconvenient times. Opportunities to love are easily missed, and this isn't just with our Beloved, but often with our family members and our friends. Love must be spontaneous, for a chance to love is not easily recovered.

The Beloved's approach isn't one of compulsion. He doesn't drive us, but rather, He draws us. Even though the Shulamite had made herself comfortable and had no intention of stirring, her Beloved hopes that He can arouse an appetite and evoke a response from her. He calls her, using all of His pet names. He reminds her of how He sees her, and then describes how she will find Him if she will only rise to greet Him.

It is also a shadow of the relationship of the Church with the King: an illustration of genuine longing in the Groom's absence. It also points to the uncomfortable fact that many come to a place of contentment in their walk with the Beloved. It seems easy to become content, just having been with Him, and then neglect the opportunities that come to us to rise and embrace Him afresh and anew.

The Beloved isn't after a onetime fling or a one-night-stand, nor will He tolerate a distracted lover. He's looking for renewed and fresh affections every day.

After a momentary delay the Shulamite rose and went to the door. She gripped the lock and opened it to find that the Shepherd-King had already gone away. Only His fragrance remained.

What terrible loss! She had been lying content in her chamber. Her dreams about Him were satisfying, but dreams aren't enough. She needed to be with Him.

Missing His call, distant in her dream world, she is like

many believers. She wasn't prepared! It's easy to dream life away, and when the opportunity comes for true relationship, for true love, lose it to hesitation or indisposition.

Having known Him once isn't enough. We cannot depend on an old familiar relationship. Losing Him will be the likely outcome. Rising a moment too late could mean losing the opportunity to know Him afresh.

Several years ago I was preparing for a service, and I heard the Holy Spirit ask: "Will you run, be a spectator, or commit yourself?" With these questions came an overwhelming sense of the gravity of this hour, the urgency of this time, and I became instantly aware of the choices. Lack of preparation, sitting around as a spectator, won't work anymore. As the Day of the Lord approaches, there is no time to waste. He is looking for unquestionably committed believers – those whose sole desire is to know Him.

> *It was but a little that I passed from them, but I FOUND HIM WHOM MY SOUL LOVETH: I HELD HIM, AND WOULD NOT LET HIM GO, until I had brought him into my mother's house, and into the chamber of her that conceived me.*   Song of Solomon 3:4

The Shulamite found her beloved after many trials, and declared, "I will never let him go." Those who find Him, whose soul's desire has been to experience the Beloved, will understand her emotion and will agree with her statement. Those who would receive all His benefits must never let Him go. He is not looking for those who seek Him – only to let Him go again. He will not be watching any schedule but His own, and He may come at what seems to you a most inconvenient time.

Upon finding Him, the Shulamite determined to take Him home. At first glance it sounds great, doesn't it? But

In the beginning of the book I mentioned an instance when the Holy Spirit spoke to me, "I've moved in, and I'm having a garage sale!" When we want to take our Beloved home with us, we have to be willing to make some changes. Taking Him home means that He moves in and takes control, and He may say, of all of those little keepsakes, and all of those useless things that have seemed so precious to us, "These all have to go." This is painful for some.

The Bride must not keep anything that could affect the intimate union in the inner chamber. She will have sought Him, she will have held Him, and she will have determined that she will never let go of Him. She has invited Him to invade every area of her life. She has nothing to hide from Him and she has nothing that He cannot touch. She is consumed with His presence and nothing else matters:

> *Thy lips, O MY SPOUSE, drop as the honeycomb: honey and milk are under thy tongue; and the smell of thy garments is like the smell of Lebanon.*
>
> Song of Solomon 4:11

The words, *"o my spouse,"* are translated from the Hebrew word, *"kallah,"* which is frequently translated "bride" in many other Old Testament passages. In our modern understanding, "bride" is used to speak of a newlywed female, but "spouse," to speak of those that have been married for sometime. In Solomon's Song, the Shulamite is to the Beloved a *"bride."*

Kallah comes from the word *"kalal,"* which means "complete" or "perfect one," the sense being that a man requires a woman to be complete. The bride makes the groom complete, and therefore, she perfects him.

Fixed Eyes

The bride of the Scriptures is different from that of our Western culture. For instance, the Middle Eastern bride got ready and then awaited the entrance of her groom, while in our Western culture, it's the groom who prepares first and then anxiously awaits the arrival of the bride. This difference in tradition can cause errors in our interpretation of certain scripture passages and, as a result, the revelation of the Bride is often misunderstood.

In the Western wedding ceremony, the music begins, and the groom enters. He then patiently waits while the wedding party makes its entrance. Finally the music changes to a note of declaration: *Here Comes the Bride*. The bride is beautiful, and her gaze is fixed on her groom.

Scripture paints a slightly different picture:

> *Let us be glad and rejoice, and give honour to him: for the marriage of the Lamb is come, and his wife hath made herself ready. And to her was granted that she should be ARRAYED IN FINE LINEN, CLEAN AND WHITE: for the fine linen is the righteousness of saints*   Revelation 19:7-8

Initially these verses may seem to point to a ceremony like the Western one just described, but if we look closely at scripture we find that the bride makes herself ready by keeping her garments clean (see Revelation 16:15). She has prepared her lamp with clean oil and trimmed her wick. She has then waited patiently for the entrance of her bridegroom.

When the Groom sees his Bride, He looks deeply into Her eyes and notes that she has eyes only for Him, or *"doves' eyes"* as Solomon described it (Song of Solomon 1:14-16). Doves' eyes are large and round, but they have no peripheral vision. They see only one thing one at a time. They are focused.

Seekers of His Face

When the Beloved, the Heavenly Bridegroom, sees that the members of the Bride have kept their vessels and made themselves ready, then, and only then, will He bestow upon her the honor of being called His wife. She will be dressed in *fine linen, clean and white,* which is *the righteousness of the saints.* For the bride to approach Him, dressed in anything else, not having prepared her heart, would be to approach Him in filthy rags (see Isaiah 64:6).

Believers who seek the intimate relationship reserved for the Bride must yearn for more than a casual or superficial encounter. They must desire a relationship that makes them call out, *"Let Him kiss me with the kisses of His mouth."* They must be prepared for a face-to-face meeting and an intimacy of superb sensations, *"for thy love is better than wine."* Such a relationship, and such preparation, will lead them to the throne — eyes fixed upon Him.

CHAPTER ELEVEN

JOSEPH'S PREPARATION

O ye seed of Israel his servant, ye children of Jacob, his chosen ones. He is the LORD our God; his judgments are in all the earth. BE YE MIND-FUL ALWAYS OF HIS COVENANT; the word which he commanded to a thousand generations; Even of the COV-ENANT WHICH HE MADE WITH ABRAHAM, and of his oath unto Isaac; And hath confirmed the same to Jacob for a law, and to Israel for AN EVERLASTING COV-ENANT, 1 Chronicles 16:13-17

As Abraham's descendants, the people of Israel were inheritor's of his promise. God promised the children of Israel, through His covenants, a land in which they could dwell, blessings and victory over their enemies, and especially, the promise of divine relationship. They only needed to have faith and obey Him to receive His promise.

During the history of Israel, there was a certain man by the name of Jacob. God changed the name of Jacob, Abraham's grandson, to Israel. Jacob had many sons, but he loved one of them, Joseph, *"more than all of his children"* and showed his love by giving his son a *"coat of many colors"* (Genesis 37:3). The coat was a symbol of great love, honor, and inheritance. Joseph would have worn it as a mark of favor and distinction. This, however, sowed a seed of jealousy and hatred in his brothers, and they conspired against him and sold him to the Midianites, who in turn took him to Egypt and sold him there (see Genesis 37:19-28).

Despite his desperate situation, Joseph soon found himself in charge of an Egyptian home, that of Potiphar. Joseph's presence brought prosperity to the entire household. But because Joseph was handsome, Potiphar's wife began to take a personal interest in him, and he was forced to flee her advances. Infuriated that he would spurn her advances, Potiphar's wife falsely accused Joseph of attacking her, and Potiphar had him thrown into prison. In all of this, God was setting the stage to elevate Joseph in the kingdom and to help Israel through a coming famine.

While Joseph was in prison, Pharaoh was having trouble with his butler and his baker, and threw them into the same prison. Little did Joseph know that these men would provide for him a way out of his prison and a way into the household of the most powerful man in the known world.

One day Joseph noticed that something was troubling the butler and the baker, so he asked them what had caused their grief. They told him that they had both dreamed unusual dreams and could find no one to interpret the dreams. Each man carefully explained his dream, and Joseph listen to every detail. Having heard their dreams, he then gave them the interpretation of each: the butler would receive full restoration, but the baker would be executed. Three days later, exactly as Joseph had predicted, Pharaoh ordered his butler restored and his baker to be hanged.

Joseph had asked the butler to remember him when he returned to the house of Pharaoh, but the butler forgot his promise, and Joseph spent two more years in jail.

Joseph's Preparation

God's times and workings are often quite different from what we think they should be. We have such limited understanding and perception of things, but God considers every detail. Sometimes it's hard for us to submit to God's program. Time in prison isn't an easy thing, especially if one knows they have done nothing wrong.

"How could this be God's perfect will?" some would ask. But Joseph trusted God and submitted to Him in everything he did. And, even in prison, God blessed and prospered him.

Joseph wasn't just anybody. He would one day hold the fate of entire nations in his hands, and especially that of Israel. God had to give him very specific preparation. Prison, though very difficult, was part of that preparation. Scripture doesn't tell us what lessons Joseph learned there, but when he emerged, he ruled and governed with wisdom and divine strength.

During Joseph's stay in prison, Pharaoh had several dreams. So alarmed was the king by these dreams that he searched for someone who could interpret them, but he could find no one. It was then, however, that the butler remembered the man in prison who had interpreted his dream. As a result, Pharaoh sent for Joseph. The lad was hastily brought before him, and Joseph was able to interpret Pharaoh's dreams, giving all the glory to God. Pharaoh wanted to honor him:

> *And the thing was good in the eyes of Pharaoh, and in the eyes of all his servants. And Pharaoh said unto his servants, CAN WE FIND SUCH A ONE AS THIS IS, A MAN IN WHOM THE SPIRIT OF GOD IS? And Pharaoh said unto Joseph, Forasmuch as God hath shewed thee all this, there is none so discreet and wise as thou art: Thou shalt be over my house, and ACCORDING UNTO THY WORD SHALL ALL MY PEOPLE BE RULED: only in the throne will I be greater than thou. And Pharaoh said*

*unto Joseph, See, I have set thee over all the land of Egypt.
And Pharaoh took off his ring from his hand, and put it
upon Joseph's hand, and arrayed him in vestures of fine
linen, and put a gold chain about his neck;*

Genesis 41:37-42

Joseph had explained that there would be seven years of plenty, followed by seven years of famine, and he encouraged Pharaoh not to worry, but to store up, and make provision during the years of plenty so that they would be no lack during the lean years. After hearing Joseph's interpretation, Pharaoh decided that the man was wiser than his own aides, so he ordered that he not be returned to the prison but be given lodging in the royal courts. Joseph was placed in charge of all of Egypt's granaries. Pharaoh gave him a wife and, in time, two sons were born to him: Mannaseh and Ephraim.

Seven years of prosperity came and went. Then seven of the worst years in history came upon them, in which the plenty was quickly devoured. All the surrounding nations were affected and the people were forced to leave their homes and buy grain in Egypt.

Jacob and his sons were also affected by the famine, and Jacob sent his sons to purchase grain from Egypt. Little could they have imagined that they would come face to face with the same boy they had sold into slavery more than twenty years earlier, and that same boy would stand before them as their governor, just as his dreams had foretold.

When Jacob's other sons saw Joseph, they didn't recognize him, but he recognized them, and a portion of his youthful dreams were fulfilled. He decided to put his brothers through several tests. Perhaps he did it to determine the condition of their hearts, or to humble them from their arrogance. There is no way to be certain of the reasons behind his decision, but he certainly taught them some serious lessons.

First, Joseph accused his brothers of being spies and threw them into prison. On the third day, he called for them and told them that he could no longer hold them because he feared God. He offered to release them on one condition – that they return with their younger brother.

In that moment, the brothers must have felt the weight of conscience heavily upon them. They felt certain that they were being tried because of what they had done to Joseph years before and they feared that the blood of their brother was about to return upon them. They were right, but not in the way they imagined. In fear, they rushed home and told their father everything that had happened to them in Egypt and everything that the governor had spoken.

Jacob, when he heard all that his sons told him, refused to send Benjamin, fearing that he, too, would be lost. But with the passing of time, the food supply began to run out, and the sons were forced to speak with their father about this matter once again. Judah vowed to be responsible for his brother Benjamin while they traveled, assuring Jacob that no harm would come to him. Jacob finally agreed and sent his sons with fine gifts for the governor of Egypt.

Joseph saw his brothers coming in the distance and planned his strategy. When they arrived, he promptly invited them in. In time the brothers presented the gifts they were carrying at Joseph's feet, just as he had seen in his dreams when he was still a boy.

When dinner time came, Joseph invited his brothers to stay as his guests. During the meal, he put his brothers to one final test. He ordered his servants to place a silver cup in Benjamin's grain bag. The next day, the brothers departed, carrying with them the silver cup hidden in the sack. As part of the plan, Joseph sent one of his servants to retrieve the cup and so test their loyalty to their younger brother.

Perhaps Joseph needed to see if they would fail Benjamin, just as they had failed him. The brothers, however, had learned their lesson and were quick to defend their younger brother. They pleaded with Joseph for the boy's safe return. As Judah rehearsed in the ears of Joseph his vow to their father, Joseph was overcome with emotion and sent all the servants out the room. In that emotion-filled moment, he revealed his identity to his brothers. He assured them that he had forgiven them and that no harm would come to them. He then offered to take care of them in the land of Egypt. God had readied the stage for His people to walk in the fullness of their inheritance.

At first, Jacob was hesitant to believe all that his sons told him upon their return, but eventually he accepted it and made preparations to travel to Egypt. Before Jacob left for Egypt, God spoke to him through four visions, confirming in his ears the faithfulness of the Lord. First God promised: *I will make out of you a great nation;* second, *I will go with you to Egypt;* third, *I will bring you out of Egypt* and fourth, *Joseph will close your eyes.* It surely comforted Israel to know that the Lord would bless him, even though he was to die in a strange land.

Joseph had prepared himself well and had become a savior to his people.

Preparation in the life of a believer is a necessary element we must encounter if we are to fulfill any capacity of use. Whether you or I are to be a water vessel or the governor holding the fate of an entire nation, God's law of preparation is the same. God's unique law of preparation specifically molds and forms the character of the vessel. It is necessary for you and I to embrace God's dealings, strippings, and washings for there is a work to be done.

PART III:

SEEKING HIS HAND? OR HIS FACE?

CHAPTER TWELVE

DELIVERANCE FROM EGYPT

*A*nd they sinned yet more against him by provoking the most High in the wilderness. And THEY TEMPTED GOD IN THEIR HEART by asking meat for their lust. Yea, they spake against God; they said, Can God furnish a table in the wilderness? Behold, he smote the rock, that the waters gushed out, and the streams overflowed; can he give bread also? can he provide flesh for his people?
Psalm 78:17-20

From the very beginning God showed His heart toward mankind, and He still longs for a people with whom He may commune and with whom He may dwell. Even the final words recorded in the Bible make it apparent that His heart is still inclined toward Adam's seed (see Revelation 22:20-21).

In His desire to have a people of His very own, called by His name and by no other, God initiated several covenants, all designed to draw man into divine relationship. These covenants were God's vehicle of expression, by which He displayed His will, His purpose, His grace and His promise to mankind.

Nothing that God does is without purpose and order.

Seekers of His Face

He has a plan, and His intervention in the affairs of humankind isn't without purpose. That intention has ushered in redemption's promise and the covenants that lead to it.

Each covenant – eight of them in all – brought the promise of redemption, fellowship, and union with God. Each revealed God's heart toward humanity and the need of every individual for redemption.

The past covenants are: the Edenic Covenant, given to man before his fall; the Adamic Covenant, given after man's fall; the Noahic Covenant, made with Noah after the flood; the Abrahamic Covenant, specifically involving Israel, but also containing the promise of Messiah for all believers; the Mosaic Covenant, established with the children of Israel after their Exodus from Egypt; the Palestinian Covenant, made with the second generation that left Egypt, after forty years of wandering; the Davidic Covenant, including the promise of an eternal throne. The New Covenant was made with the twelve disciples (and, through them, with all believers) just before Jesus' death. It fulfilled all previous covenants. Then there is the Everlasting Covenant, which will be made in eternity, the consummation of all previous covenants, involving God's eternal purpose toward man. No one covenant was complete in itself. They all worked together to make up the whole of redemption's plan.

Covenant is not a word easily understood by our modern culture. In our parents' time, a man's word was as good as a handshake, and nothing more was needed for commercial interchanges of land and livestock. Today, promises are broken as easily as sticks. People no longer approach each other with compassion, respect, reverence, or commitment. There seems to be nothing that obliges them to keep their word toward God, much less with anyone else. All respect for the meaning of covenant, therefore, seems to have evaporated.

How many times have I heard people say that they are no longer under the Law, and thus, no longer obligated to keep the covenants that bound Israel? But this is not true. All the previous covenants pointed to the coming of the Messiah and His promise of redemption. Therefore, when Jesus came, He didn't abolish the Law, but fulfilled it.

Associated with each covenant were acts (for example, circumcision, as part of the Abrahamic Covenant) that now find their fulfillment in spiritual principles. At the cross, Jesus fulfilled circumcision, and replaced it with circumcision of the heart – an eternal seal (see Romans 2:25-29).

All the elements and acts that made up the Law now find their fulfillment in the Eternal Covenant, in Jesus. Because of Him and His work believers are united with the greatest covenant and made partakers of an everlasting inheritance! Being joined to God, the believer is melded to all that pertains to godliness, not the part of God they like. This includes His laws, as well as His blessings. Under the Everlasting Covenant, God's people must not forget or neglect those laws established through His covenants.

As important as God's law is, however, His Church is made a part of Him by grace. Therefore, the fulfillment of His promises is no longer based on carnal works, but on works of faith, trust, and belief.

An examination, in greater depth, of the word "covenant" is in order. A "covenant" is *a binding agreement between two or more parties which ends with either its fulfillment or by the death of one of the parties.*" According to *Strong's Concordance*, the Hebrew word translated covenant is *"beriyth."* This word means, "a compact (because it is made by passing between pieces of flesh)." Thus, covenant meant "cutting":

> *And it came to pass, that, when the sun went down, and it was dark, behold a smoking furnace, and a burning lamp that PASSED BETWEEN those pieces. In the same day the LORD made a covenant with Abram, saying, Unto thy seed have I given this land, from the river of Egypt unto the great river, the river Euphrates:* Genesis 15:17-18

When God approaches a covenant, He joins Himself to it by "cutting." First, He makes an oath, which is His word, and, secondly, He seals that oath with the shedding of blood.

A covenant may contain conditions, terms, promises, blessings, curses, and warnings. The conditions of God's covenants are simple, requiring only faith and obedience. Since God has initiated them, He alone has the ability and authority to see to it that the promises are effective and are fulfilled. The only responsibility for the recipient is to believe.

God's purpose in using covenants was to demonstrate certain truths to His people. First, He was a covenant-making God. Secondly, He was a covenant-keeping God (see Deuteronomy 7:9). And thirdly, He was a covenant-revealing God (see Psalm 25:14).

God took the initiative and declared His desire toward mankind, but without the covenant's revelation none would know His desires. With every covenant, God demonstrated His divine nature. He established Himself as a God of promise, fulfillment, enablement, and redemption.

God, having joined Himself to a covenant, declared that

Deliverance From Egypt

He would not neglect or forget it, and He encouraged Israel to do the same.

Every covenant brought the promise of blessing, but only if the people of God would set their eyes upon Him and seek His face and look beyond what they saw with their natural eyes.

A look at the children of Israel during their captivity in Egypt, their journey in the wilderness, and their entrance into the promised land gives important instruction in this matter.

When Jacob arrived in Egypt with all of his extended family, Pharaoh gave him the land of Goshen as a place to dwell. There Israel prospered and multiplied, just as prophecy had foretold.

After Joseph died, another Pharaoh came to power who feared Israel's prosperity and slowly began stripping the Jews of all rights and privileges, forcing them into slavery. Soon, the descendants of Abraham found themselves in cruel bondage. God knew that this would happen and had already made provision for their deliverance.

Bondage never happens overnight. It happens gradually, like night overtaking day.

When I was a child, my parents made a rule that when the street lights came on, it was time for us to be inside. It seemed like an easy rule to follow, but when children get busy playing chase, they lose all concept of time. When a familiar voice called, "It's time to come in," invariably I answered, "But it's not even dark yet."

Of course it was dark, and the street lights had come on sometime before, but I'd been so busy playing that I didn't realize how dark it had gotten. After I had gone inside and turned to look back out the door, from brilliance to darkness, night's black veil seemed to have abruptly hedged in upon what had been, only moments before, the intensity of day. It really hadn't happened as quickly as I thought. It just appeared so. Night's obscurity was now contrasted against the light inside.

While in Egypt, the children of Israel not only lost their freedom, but they lost their vision of God. They strayed from their belief in God and began worshipping the idols of Egypt (see Ezekiel 20:8).

Believers must never bow to Egypt's false gods. Those who have received Jesus no longer belong to the kingdom of darkness (see 2 Corinthians 6:16-18). They are no longer citizens of this world.

Sometimes human reasoning is useful in justifying compromise. "You have to get along," some say. "Don't make waves. You're in Egypt, do as the Egyptians do."

Israel compromised her standards and began to tolerate a worldly mixture, and bondage was the result. Sadly, such bondage was necessary to prepare the children of Israel for deliverance, and so, God promised them that a deliverer would come.

During Israel's bondage, Pharaoh made a decree that the midwives must kill every male child born to Abraham's seed. But some of the midwives feared God and refused to carry out Pharaoh's command.

Pharaoh then employed another means of destroying the Hebrew babies, ordering that the newborns be thrown into the Nile. During this time a young woman from the house of Levi bore a son. She hid him three months until it was no longer possible, and then she prepared a basket to float him in the river.

It happened that Pharaoh's daughter was bathing that day along the Nile, and the basket came floating near her among the bulrushes. Upon retrieving the basket, she found a tiny baby hidden inside. She had no way of knowing it, but she had just played an important part in providing a savior for Israel from the tyranny and bondage of Egypt.

This child, Moses, saved from the waters of the vast Nile and reared in Pharaoh's court, grew to be a man and, though poor of speech, became God's head of state and a prophet. He had much to overcome in his past, having been fished out of a big river as an abandoned child, and forty years of exile, most of which was spent tending a flock of sheep. His resume probably would not have impressed many.

Moses probably had an excellent education, but his speech impediment may have made him incapable of any leadership role or office. He wasn't sure of his own ability. *"O my Lord,"* he cried, *"I am not eloquent. ... I am slow of speech."* He thought God should have sent someone else (see Exodus 4:10-14).

Did God make a mistake in choosing Moses? What about others that God has appointed and commissioned? Were they any better?

King David? He was good at killing giants, but he turned out to be an adulterer and a murderer. Many editorials would have probably commented: "Better a prison than a palace," for this man, and his approval rating would have plummeted to an abysmal low on certain occasions. At one point, his men even spoke of stoning him (see 1 Samuel 30:6).

And Saul? Later known as Paul, he was highly educated, definitely leadership material, but his main claim to fame upon entering public life was his role as a zealot – "wasting" Christians in the most convenient way.

It would have been hard to see anything good in Saul, especially if you were one of the martyrs that he helped make famous.

But God saw that Moses would extend his rod, and

the Red Sea would part. God saw that David had a heart after His own. God knew that Saul would become Paul. Our God looks through knowing eyes, full of wisdom, abundant grace, and deep-felt mercy, to see the glory that a surrendered life will bring to Him.

Reading Exodus makes us aware of just how true this is. Again, to human eyes, it would seem that God must have chosen the wrong people. They were stubborn and stiff-necked. They often fell away completely, even to the point of seeking other gods and dancing around a golden calf. In the wilderness their hearts were proven, and they failed, again and again, failure upon failure. But God never gave up on them. Each failure was an opportunity for Him to show Himself as God, and a time for His glory to be seen in His people and through His work in them (see Deuteronomy 8:2-3 and 15-18).

Moses seemed to know that his assignment would be difficult. He was concerned that Israel would not accept him (see Exodus 3:13). God also knew that conquering Israel's hearts would prove far more challenging than conquering Pharaoh. So Moses was first sent to the elders of Israel. God sent him with three messages: first, to assure Israel that God had seen all that the Egyptians had done to them; secondly, that He would surely bring them out of the land of affliction; and third, that He would bring them to a land flowing with milk and honey.

Moses again expressed concern and said, *"They will not believe me, nor hearken unto my voice,"* (Exodus 4:1) Regrettably, Moses's concerns were valid. Israel did have trouble believing, but God provided Moses with three signs that would prove his divine mandate. He could use one sign, or all three, depending on how many signs were needed to convince the people. First, he was to throw down his rod, and it would turn into a serpent. Secondly, he could put his hand in his coat and then remove it and it would be leprous. Upon returning the hand to his coat and removing it, it would be clean again. Third, he could turn water into blood.

Moses did as the Lord commanded him, calling the elders of Israel together and telling them what the Lord had spoken. I wish I could say that Israel believed by simply hearing the Lord's word, but she didn't. Not only did the children of Israel not easily listen to Moses, but one sign wasn't enough for them. They needed all three. Israel sought God's hand, but not His face. She sought what His hand could give them, but a seeker of His face seeks Him for Who He is and for His presence.

Before the children of Israel left Egypt, God gave them an illustration of His promised deliverance. He told them to pay attention and to remember, for it would be a sign of His faithfulness. Not only would their deliverance be the result of wondrous miracles, but it would also be a shadow pointing to their coming Deliverer.

Moses instructed all of Israel to take a lamb for every household and if their number was too small for a whole lamb, they were to share one with their neighbors. God ordained the institution of the Passover in remembrance of Israel's great deliverance from Egyptian bondage. That month would become the first month of the Hebrew calendar. On the tenth day, they would take a lamb without blemish, a male of the first year, and after keeping it a brief time, kill it on the fourteenth day. The innocent lamb, the best one, probably the one that the children had played with, was the very one that must be sacrificed. God intended for this sacrifice to make a profound impression. Then they were to take the blood and put it on the sides and the tops of the door frames of their homes. God said:

> *Your lamb shall be without blemish, a male of the first year:*
> *ye shall take it out from the sheep, or from the goats: And*
> *ye shall keep it up until the fourteenth day of the same*
> *month: and the whole assembly of the congregation of Is-*
> *rael shall kill it in the evening. AND THEY SHALL TAKE*
> *OF THE BLOOD, AND STRIKE IT ON THE TWO SIDE*
> *POSTS AND ON THE UPPER DOOR POST OF THE*
> *HOUSES, wherein they shall eat it. And they shall eat the*
> *flesh in that night, roast with fire, and unleavened bread;*
> *and with bitter herbs they shall eat it.*   Exodus 12:5-8

The houses that had been *"covered"* by the lamb's blood were delivered from God's judgment upon the firstborn of each family:

> *And it came to pass, that at midnight the LORD smote all*
> *the firstborn in the land of Egypt, from the firstborn of*
> *Pharaoh that sat on his throne unto the firstborn of the*
> *captive that was in the dungeon; and all the firstborn of*
> *cattle. And Pharaoh rose up in the night, he, and all his*
> *servants, and all the Egyptians; and there was a great cry*
> *in Egypt; FOR THERE WAS NOT A HOUSE WHERE*
> *THERE WAS NOT ONE DEAD.*   Exodus 12:29-30

Through this last great plague, Israel was delivered. It presents to us a beautiful representation of God's plan for redemption. As the lamb brought deliverance to each home that identified itself with the slain lamb, so does Jesus today. As the lamb brought freedom from bondage for a nation, so, too, Jesus for His Church, *"an holy nation"* (see 1 Peter 2:9).

It is great to know that God never leaves any of His promises unfulfilled. You can count on it. He always completely accomplishes His Word. He is a God of promise, a

Deliverance From Egypt

God of fulfillment, but He will not sidestep His order. He is God and things must be done His way. He is also not a halfway God (see Isaiah 55:11).

The land of Egypt, although it was a land of Gentiles, was God's instrument to work redemption and promise in Israel. Egypt would become the means that would allow God to show the children of Israel that He would be faithful to His covenants – even if they weren't. Without Egypt, and everything it represents, perhaps the distinction between those who are seekers of God's hand and those who are *Seekers of His Face* would never have been so visible.

Miraculously God dealt with Egypt, and the exodus began. The people of Israel took with them cattle, sheep, and gold and silver from Egypt. The Lord faithfully delivered them, just as He promised. He led them through a pillar of cloud by day and through a pillar of fire by night.

In the days ahead, however, it would be revealed again and again, that they were simply seekers of His hand.

CHAPTER THIRTEEN

SEEKERS OF HIS HAND

*T*herefore the LORD heard this, and was wroth: so a fire was kindled against Jacob, and anger also came up against Israel; BECAUSE THEY BE-LIEVED NOT IN GOD, AND TRUSTED NOT IN HIS SALVATION: Though he had commanded the clouds from above, and opened the doors of heaven, And had rained down manna upon them to eat, and had given them of the corn of heaven. MAN DID EAT ANGELS' FOOD: he sent them meat to the full. He caused an east wind to blow in the heaven: and by his power he brought in the south wind. He rained flesh also upon them as dust, and feathered fowls like as the sand of the sea: And he let it fall in the midst of their camp, round about their habitations. So they did eat, and were well filled: for he gave them their own desire; They were not estranged from their lust. But while their meat was yet in their mouths, The wrath of God came upon them, and slew the fattest of them, and smote down the chosen men of Israel. For all this they sinned still, and believed not for his wondrous works. Therefore their days did he consume in vanity, and their years in trouble. When he slew them, THEN THEY SOUGHT HIM: AND THEY RETURNED AND INQUIRED EARLY AFTER GOD. And they remembered that God was their rock, and the high God their redeemer. Nevertheless they did flatter him with

*their mouth, and they lied unto him with their tongues.
FOR THEIR HEART WAS NOT RIGHT WITH HIM,
NEITHER WERE THEY STEDFAST IN HIS COV-
ENANT. But he, being full of compassion, forgave their
iniquity, and destroyed them not: yea, many a time turned
he his anger away, and did not stir up all his wrath. FOR
HE REMEMBERED THAT THEY WERE BUT FLESH;
a wind that passeth away, and cometh not again. How oft did
they provoke him in the wilderness, and grieve him in the
desert! YEA, THEY TURNED BACK AND TEMPTED
GOD, AND LIMITED THE HOLY ONE OF ISRAEL.*

Psalm 78:21-41

The people of Israel had begun a journey that would
show what was in their hearts. Between Egypt and Sinai,
God tested their faith and their obedience with four separate trials. Each test brought promises from God, for He
wanted Israel to know that she could trust what He said,
and that He was faithful to fulfill His promises. His deepest desire was to take His people beyond their natural
sight and human understanding, to a place of absolute
trust in Him.

Shortly after the exodus began, the children of Israel
found themselves encamped by the Red Sea. Meanwhile,
back in Egypt, God hardened Pharaoh's heart and he rose
up to follow the Israelites. Again, God was setting the
stage. He would soon show Israel His faithfulness.

Because God had marked Israel, as a people, to accomplish His bidding, He must prove them. And, rest assured,
He will prove all those who choose to call Him their God.
To "prove" means *to establish as true, to establish validity or
authenticity*. A blacksmith will prove gold or silver by using heat. The true elements remain in the fire, while the
impurities surface. So when God proves us, He not only
tests, but secures those who are thus tested in their faith.

Seekers of His Hand

Pharaoh's armies were approaching and Israel would soon be tested for the first time.

Encamped near the shores of the sea, they began to hear strange sound. It wasn't thunder, and it wasn't rejoicing. It was the dreadful sound of approaching chariots. Lifting their eyes they beheld Pharaoh's armies coming after them in hot pursuit. It was a terrible sight, chariots lifting clouds of dust high in the air, and the people of Israel fell into fear.

How quickly they forgot all the miracles God had done to bring them forth from Egypt! Their memory of the Passover and the miraculous judgments that brought them out of bondage immediately vanished, as if lost in the clouds of desert dust rising from the advancing legion. Not even the divinely sent cloud by day and fire by night — ever present signs of God's presence — kept their fear in check. Simply, they had forgotten the Word of the Lord and its meaning. And in that instant of trembling they could no longer see beyond their circumstances.

Those who seek only God's hand will find themselves continually facing difficult or impossible circumstances and needs. When one faces a need, his or her belief is being tested.

When God allows His people to face overwhelming circumstances, He is checking to see if we will have faith and trust in His Word.

The human tendency is to look for deliverance from, or deliverance out of, instead of facing up to and going through the circumstances that God has allowed for a work of perfection in His children. If the believer will take the challenge and face the situation, God has promised that He will be with us, just as He was in the cloud and the pillar of fire (see Deuteronomy 4:31).

Never forget the cloud of His glory and the fire of His Spirit. He's with those who seek Him, even in the darkest situations. That is His promise. It is His Word. He has promised to be always watching over and faithfully leading His own.

Unfortunately, life's circumstances will sometimes speak louder than the Word of the Lord, even when we know that His Word is true. Frequently, to break through a situation, the believer must make a deliberate decision to rest and trust in the promises of God. The children of Israel needed to learn this lesson, for God was about to lead them through some very difficult circumstances.

As the chariots' roar approached, the children of Israel began to murmur and complain. *Perhaps Egypt, with all its toils and hardships, wasn't so bad after all,* they thought.

All too frequently believers find themselves looking back to the bondage from which they came. At such times, the pictures that come to their minds can be pleasant ones. Of course the evil one isn't going to remind them of the bad times, when he trampled them, beat them, and wounded them. The enemy persistently uses colorful memories to remind Christians of their past and to deter them from pressing forward in faith in contrary situations.

The specialty of the evil one is creating doubt and unbelief, anything that might throw us off the path to God's blessings. He said to Eve, *"Yea, hath God said ... ?* (Genesis 3:1). Entertaining Egypt's thoughts will quickly bring unbelief, and the result is often devastating.

When the children of Israel, facing the Pharaoh's chariots, began to murmur and complain, Moses responded, *"Fear ye not, stand still, and see the salvation of the LORD, ... ye shall see them again no more for ever"* (Exodus 14:13-14).

Moses knew God and trusted His Word. He had become a seeker of God's face. He saw beyond *what* God did to *who* God was. He knew that God was more than His manifestation. He knew that God's workings were merely a shadow of His divine person. When God demonstrated, through the Passover, Israel's coming deliverance, Moses knew that the Passover represented much more than that which human eyes had seen. He knew that God *was* deliverance, and that deliverance was a part of His divine nature. Having this faith, or certainty, Moses encouraged the people to hold their peace and not to entertain Egypt's thoughts, but to trust in God for salvation.

Because Moses knew God's promises, and further, because he knew his God, and he knew that his God would back him up, he instructed the people to stand still and to watch the salvation of their Lord. Moses himself didn't know, and he didn't have to know, how the Lord would save them from Pharaoh's armies. He simply knew what the Lord had said:

> *And I have said, I WILL BRING YOU UP OUT OF the affliction of Egypt unto the land of the Canaanites, and the Hittites, and the Amorites, and the Perizzites, and the Hivites, and the Jebusites, unto a land flowing with milk and honey.* Exodus 3:17

Moses took God at His word and stood firmly in faith and obedience. God said to him:

> *But lift thou up thy rod, and STRETCH OUT THINE HAND OVER THE SEA, AND DIVIDE IT: and the children of Israel shall go on dry ground through the midst of the sea. And I, behold, I will harden the hearts of the Egyptians, and they shall follow them: and I will get me honour upon Pharaoh, and upon all his host, upon his chariots, and upon his horsemen. And the Egyptians shall know that I am the LORD, when I have gotten me honour upon Pharaoh, upon his chariots, and upon his horsemen.* Exodus 14:16-18

There was something that Moses must do. *"Lift thou up thy rod,"* God instructed him, *"stretch out thine hand over the sea, and divide it."* And when Moses obeyed, God caused a strong east wind to blow which moved back the sea exposing a dry path through which the Israelites could pass. Then, with another movement of his hand, Moses, in obedience to God, caused the waters to come crashing back upon the doomed armies of Pharaoh.

In dividing the Red Sea, God was establishing two important truths. First, He was indicating that he would fight for His people, and second, their enemies would soon be no more.

It is the Lord's desire that His people walk forward in complete victory, not only victory in their momentary need or circumstances, but also in victory from slavery. When God brings His people through a trial of faith, He wants to place them on dry land. His people will walk upright with nothing bogging them down or tying them to their past. They will have to overcome many obstacles. By defeating the Egyptians, God showed them that he could conquer the enemy of their past and the enemy of their present circumstances.

The second test which the people of Israel faced came when Moses brought them out of the wilderness of Migdol and into the wilderness of Shur:

> *And when they came to Marah, they could not drink of the waters of Marah, for they were bitter: therefore the name of it was called Marah. AND THE PEOPLE MUR-MURED AGAINST MOSES, saying, What shall we drink?* Exodus 15:23-24

Only three days into the wilderness, Israel faced a water shortage. The people came to the waters of Marah, thinking that they had solved their problem, but the waters were bitter.

Considering the many miracles that had brought them to this point, one would think, *"Well Israel, you know, just trust God. He'll get you through this, just like He got you through everything else."* But the children of Israel murmured, instead. Water, which God had effectively used for their deliverance, now became an instrument of testing and a subject about which to complain and murmur later.

In Marah the Lord wanted to show again His faithfulness to deliver His people from difficulties of staggering magnitude. There He established a statute and an ordinance. He wanted them to remember that even the most bitter waters, when touched by His hand, would turn sweet. By using a tree as the instrument for healing the waters, God was pointing them to Calvary.

How bitter, and how sorrowful, are some of the waters we find in this fallen world! But Calvary's tree can make them sweet. If sorrow, disappointment, rejection, or hurt has grown in your heart, making life a bitter pool of undrinkable water, God has rivers of living water for you. And if His living waters already flow from our lives, He would have us to search out the needy and give them a drink as well.

Unforgiveness can quickly pollute a fresh spring, and once the water is spoiled, nothing can change it, save Calvary's tree, which turns the bitter to sweet, making ruined lives new and fresh.

At Marah, God joined Himself to Israel with a promise. If Israel would keep His commandments and listen to His voice, then God vowed to keep them from all disease. God was establishing truths that would carry Israel through her entire journey. She was learning firsthand that

God was her provider and the He would be her healer.

God continued with His endeavor, determined to see if the children of Israel would look beyond what He did and see Him as their personal God. He performed every miracle and every provision in a way that revealed His nature and character. He hoped that Israel would seek His face, not just His hand. The entire experience was a training ground, both for Israel and for us.

God had delivered Israel from Egypt at the Red Sea and had now given sweet waters to drink and the promise of healing. By now God's people were surely secure and content. They hit the road again and came upon the twelve wells of Elim. Not only were there twelve wells, but also *"threescore and ten"* (seventy) palm trees. This must have been a welcome sight for those weary travelers.

While they made camp under the palm trees and refreshed themselves, the third test came to them. They once again began to hear a sound. This time it was not the sound of the enemy chariots but the sound of their hungry bellies. So what did they do? It seems that by now they would have learned to call on God, but no, they murmured and complained again, showing what was in their hearts:

> *And the children of Israel said unto them, WOULD TO GOD WE HAD DIED BY THE HAND OF THE LORD in the land of Egypt, when we sat by the flesh pots, and when we did eat bread to the full; for ye have brought us forth into this wilderness, to kill this whole assembly with hunger.* Exodus 16:3

The people of Israel still had appetites for Egypt. After all of God's miracles, they hungered for *the flesh pots*, and that hunger clouded their vision. The Promised Land was so far away, before them lie only a desert wilderness, and behind them was Egypt.

This time it was not their enemy which was robbing them of their trust in God, but the grumbling of their own flesh. Again they were allowing circumstances to rob them of God's blessing. They wanted the promise, but the road wasn't what they had expected, and soon they were murmuring, complaining, and doubting God's promises.

Many times I've heard people say, "God said ... ," but the moment contrary and unexpected circumstances arise, they do exactly the opposite of what God has spoken to them. I don't know whether this breaks my heart more, or simply makes me altogether angry — perhaps both.

When God's people change their tune from what God said, it makes God look fickle, as if He had changed His mind.

We hear so many times out of our emotions or need and we convince ourselves that we have heard the voice of God. There are many voices, one of which is the human spirit, and it can often be the loudest voice, especially if we are in turmoil or confusion at the moment. It is for this reason that God has placed within His Body leaders to help clarify the many voices that speak to us. No one likes to be told that they have not heard from God, but in many cases, emotions and circumstances prevent clarity concerning these matters, so we need that help.

Israel needed a change of diet. Their tastes had grown accustomed to leeks and garlic, but God had a different food in mind for them – Heaven's food. God told Moses that He would cause it to rain bread from Heaven and that if His people would obey His instructions they would have plenty to eat:

And in the morning the dew lay round about the host. And

> *when the dew that lay was gone up, behold, upon the face of the wilderness there lay a small round thing, as small as the hoar frost on the ground. And when the children of Israel saw it, they said one to another, IT IS MANNA: for they wist not what it was. And Moses said unto them, This is the bread which the LORD hath given you to eat.*
>
> Exodus 16:13-15

After the dew came, manna appeared. Dew is a sign of refreshing. This is an expressive picture of God's Word as His chosen source of refreshment and sustenance for His people.

About a year ago I was attending a conference. As I was enjoying the praise and worship, I heard God's voice ask, "Will your worship sustain you?" As I stood pondering His question, its directness and importance rang loud and clear in my heart. When we come before Him in true worship, we feast upon Who He is. In those moments, one may fill themselves with His sustaining attributes and be completely satisfied in who He is.

The Shulamite said:

> *Because of the savour of thy good ointments thy name is as ointment poured forth, therefore do the virgins love thee.*
>
> Song of Songs 1:3

The Shulamite, lost in the arms of her Beloved, was satisfied just by His smell and His shadow. She did not look to the banqueting house. That's easy. That is His hand. She sought something higher, Who He was – smell and shadow. He wanted them to learn to look at Him. He was the manna from Heaven.

Moses instructed the children of Israel to gather enough manna for one day's meals. During five days they were to gather just enough for each day, no more. They were not to save any for the next day. On the sixth day they could gather enough for two days so that they could rest on the seventh day.

Just as God had promised, manna came from Heaven, and the people went to gather. Instead of gathering just enough for one day, however, as they had been instructed, some collected enough for a much longer period. When they awoke the next day, they found that worms had spoiled the portion they kept overnight.

This act of disobedience angered Moses, and he spoke to them again, commanding that they should gather only a single day's portion each of the five days. This time the children of Israel did as Moses had instructed.

Everyone wondered what would happen on the day they gathered extra, but on the seventh day, when they awoke, they found that there were no worms to spoil the manna they had gathered the day before. God's Word was true.

The next week, things didn't go as smoothly. When the sixth day came, some of the people didn't gather enough for the seventh. Rising the next day, they went out to gather manna and found nothing. The Lord was angered by their insolence and asked them, *"How long refuse ye to keep my commandments and my laws?"* (Exodus 16:28). In Egypt Israel had grown accustomed to lawlessness, embracing Egyptian idolatry and neglecting the laws and the worship of Jehovah. Compromise had infiltrated their beliefs and their worship.

In our world today, there is a strong tendency toward compromise, and consequently many churches have suffered. Many people feel that they get better advice from TV talk shows than they get from the pulpit of their church. Some churches go so far as to hold Saturday night services so that people don't have to get out of bed on Sunday morning. Ministers in some churches pipe their messages to car windows through curb-side speakers so that people don't have to get out of their cars when they go to church. And then there are the "Light Clubs," where professing Christians sip wine and listen to contemporary Christian music. Reader's Digest sermons produced by computer-generated files are replacing ministers falling on their faces seeking God for His Word.

Certainly, wicked times are upon us, and one can sense urgency in the air. I sometimes wish that I could climb to the highest rooftop and cry aloud, "It's high time to wake up":

> *And that, knowing the time, that now it is high time to awake out of sleep: for now is our salvation nearer than when we believed. THE NIGHT IS FAR SPENT, THE DAY IS AT HAND: let us therefore CAST OFF THE WORKS OF DARKNESS, and let us put on the armour of light.* Romans 13:11-12

If indeed we are blood-bought children of the Most High, we should look different, act different, and smell different. We should walk in the character and in the image of the One who called us. We should walk, not after the desires of the flesh. Rather, a fragrance of myrrh — an air of brokenness and humility — should fill the abodes we enter.

God's objective was to use the wilderness to change His people's walk, their appetite, and their belief. He wanted them to learn to trust Him in any situation. There was a promised land to occupy and possess, but they had to be ready to conquer its giants. For that, they would need a new vision. And the wilderness was their training ground.

The fourth test came at Rephidim (see Exodus 17:1-3). It was a final test to see if the people would keep God's ordinance that He had given them at Marah. Again they found themselves without water.

Surely by now, the children of Israel should have gotten the picture. Delivered at the Red Sea, Marah's bitter waters sweetened, bread from Heaven, not to mention little things like clothing and shoes that didn't wear out (see Deuteronomy 8:2-5) – they should have realize by that time that a faithful God was helping them every step of the way. But did they? No! A moment of thirst soon left the Israelites murmuring again.

It is amazing how loud our bodies will speak to us when they are deprived. David was aware of this problem and left us a sound principle to use to dominate our flesh. He talked to his body, to his soul, to his thoughts, and to his emotions. And he directly commanded them to get straightened out:

Why art thou cast down, O my soul? and why art thou disquieted in me? HOPE THOU IN GOD: for I shall yet praise him for the help of his countenance.   Psalm 42:5

But the Israelites in the wilderness hadn't truly listened to God and began to murmur, just as they had in every previous test. They allowed the circumstances of the moment to rob them of their hope.

God, despite their faithless hearts, commanded Moses to stretch forth his rod and strike the rock. And, when he did, water rushed forth to meet their need. It was upon the Rock, they were to put their trust. We, in the face of life's trials, can trust if we build our trust upon a sure foundation – the Rock, Who is Jesus Christ, our Lord.

With each test, God had sought to turn Israel's heart

away from Egypt and toward belief in Him. He had shown himself to be their Jehovah-Jireh (provider), there Jehovah-Rapha (healer), and their Jehovah-Nissi (banner). But each failed test showed the deteriorated condition of the heart of the people. During the forty years of wandering in the wilderness they provoked God ten times (see Numbers 14:22). Several times, they recognized their failings and promised to obey the Word of the Lord (see Exodus 19:8; 24:3 and 7), but their words were empty promises, and their hearts proved faithless (see Deuteronomy 32:20).

During those forty years, the only thing the children of Israel sought was God's hand — what He could offer them. They ventured no further than their immediate need. They never sought His glory and never experienced His presence as He desired.

They saw His glory in their need and they felt His presence in difficult circumstances, but they had no desire to enter into His godliness. They were content to stand without. So near ... and yet so far.

Seeking God's hand isn't a bad thing, especially for those who have just begun to discover the things of God. But when a believer cannot get beyond seeking His hand, that believer will always be running around in the desert, facing one test after another, so close to the promised land, but never quite ready to pass over and enter their promised reward.

Before finishing this chapter, I want to take a moment to look specifically at our wilderness. We have looked at the wilderness through which Israel journeyed, but your wilderness experience can be here and now.

At one point, I had heard so many teachings on "The Wilderness Experience," that I found myself despising and rejecting anything that seemed to indicate that I was

in a wilderness myself. Then one day I found myself ready
to enter a new season in my experience with God, and I
knew that it was going to be a wilderness journey. Sobbing, I resisted, but, although I was frightened, I heard
the Lord's voice telling me to look closely at the wilderness.

I sat down with my Bible once again to read the all-
familiar account and I noticed that the wilderness was
not a solitary place, vast and dry, but rather a place where
His presence could be found in every hardship:

*WHO IS THIS THAT COMETH OUT OF THE WILDER-
NESS LIKE PILLARS OF SMOKE, perfumed with myrrh
and frankincense, with all powders of the merchant? Behold
his bed, which is Solomon's; threescore valiant men are
about it, of the valiant of Israel. They all hold swords, being expert in war: every man hath his sword upon his thigh
because of fear in the night.* Song of Solomon 3:6-8

In the dry places, I found running water. In the bitter
places there was a touch of His cross. Where there was
hunger, He satisfied it with refreshing, heavenly provi-
sions. In the solitary place, there was joy. The very place
that I had rejected for so long turned out to be a place of
hope, for with every step that Israel took, God was there.

I believe that the Body of Christ is standing on the
threshold of a new journey, just as the children of Israel
stood on the shores of the Red Sea. As we stand, facing
what's before us, we can either choose to murmur and
complain, or we can stand in revelation and in promise.

For some the wilderness awaits. Choose well, for in
the wilderness you will be proven, both your appetite and
your character. Will you perish in the desert and forfeit
your inheritance? Or will you survive the ravages of the
wilderness and move on to your promised land?

Others are already well into their wilderness journey. Be faithful and remember all the statutes and promises that God has given you. If you are thirsty, look to the Rock. If you are hungry, eat heavenly manna. If your waters have turned bitter, allow His bloodstained cross to dip in and sweeten them. And always remember: a promise of great inheritance awaits you.

Then there are those of you who have allowed God to test you and build your character. You have learned faith, trust, and obedience through the things you have suffered. And you have allowed your appetites to be changed. But your journey is not over yet. You now find yourself at the edge of yet another body of water. This time it's not the Red Sea, but the Jordan River. The word Jordan means *"to descend."* And you are about to do just that.

As you look across the river, you can barely see all God has promised you, but then a voice says:

> *Sanctify yourselves: for to morrow the LORD will do wonders among you.*   Joshua 3:5

Now you're ready to descend and wash the wilderness dust away. Everything that you are has been brought to the place of descent. Go ahead, pass through Jordan into the land of promise, without your own agenda, but with His revelation. God has imparted His presence and filled you with His person. The face you have long sought is now before you and your steps of faith will part the Jordan.

CHAPTER FOURTEEN

SEEKERS OF HIS FACE

*I f I shut up heaven that there be no rain, or if I command
the locusts to devour the land, or if I send pestilence
among my people; If my people, which are called by
my name, shall humble themselves, and pray, AND SEEK
MY FACE, and turn from their wicked ways; then will I
hear from heaven, and will forgive their sin, and will heal
their land.*   2 Chronicles 7:13-14*

God's desire has always been to find those who would
seek His face, and the prophet Elijah was such a person.
Little is know about his origins, except that he was a
Tishbite (and even scholars differ on what that might
mean). We can, however, gain valuable revelation by looking at his life and ministry.

Many know Elijah only as the prophet whom Elisha
followed and from whom he received his mantle. Obviously, there was something special about a man who could
call down fire from Heaven, as he did on several occasions, and yet he was humble enough to allow his mantle
of anointing to fall upon his apprentice.

Elisha did well to ask for the mantle of Elijah, whose
office God had chosen him to fill, and for which post he
was being groomed. God had said to Elijah, *"And Elisha
the son of Shaphat of Abelmeholah shalt thou anoint to be
prophet in thy room"* (1 Kings 19:16).

Elijah's example, as one concerned to train a successor, beautifully depicts spiritual training. From generation to generation, teaching that is not passed on to others is lost. It is up to the older generation to willingly instruct the younger, and it is up to the younger generation to be eager to learn. Unfortunately, throughout Church history, many jewels of wisdom have been lost because one generation or the other wasn't willing.

Elijah and Elisha made an ideal pair, because Elijah was willing to lead, and Elisha was willing to follow. Their hearts were joined in a singular purpose and there was a fluid expression between generations. It happened with ease, power, and anointing.

I believe that one generation should stand upon the other's shoulders, with no stepping over or around. It should be an easy transition, like a runner passing his baton to the next in line.

What was it that Elisha saw and wanted? What was it in Elijah that God would honor such a request? After all, unless God honored the request, it would have just been an old cloak tossed about his shoulders. Instead, what he sought and what he found was a double portion:

> *And Elijah took his mantle, and wrapped it together, and smote the waters, and they were divided hither and thither, so that they two went over on dry ground. And it came to pass, when they were gone over, that Elijah said unto Elisha, Ask what I shall do for thee, before I be taken away from thee. And Elisha said, I pray thee, LET A DOUBLE PORTION OF THY SPIRIT BE UPON ME.* 2 Kings 2:8-9

I truly believe that we are living in the time of Elijah (see Malachi 4:5). Jesus indicated that John the Baptist had already fulfilled a portion of this prophecy (see Matthew

17:11-13). However, in this age we yet await *the great and dreadful day of the LORD.* This indicates that Elijah's day, as prophesied by Malachi, has yet to be fulfilled in its totality.

I believe that Elijah's spirit and his call to repentance is heavy upon God's Church, calling individuals to return to their first love, drawing slothful servants to readiness, and awakening slumbering saints. The sound of repentance is being heard across the nation, returning hearts to God, and drawing backsliders home.

And even as Elijah passed his mantle and a double portion to Elisha, the day has come for the Church to expect and accept its double portion of anointing, moving boldly and supernaturally, as did Elijah:

> *And Elijah the Tishbite, who was of the inhabitants of Gilead, said unto Ahab, As the LORD God of Israel liveth, before whom I stand, there shall not be dew nor rain these years, BUT ACCORDING TO MY WORD.*
>
> 1 King 17:1

This passage points to the reason Elijah's life and ministry were successful. He was a prophet of great boldness, strength, and conviction, but his strength did not rest in his own abilities, but rather in the fact his God was alive. He said, *"As the LORD God of Israel liveth ... ,"* for he knew that his God was alive and well, siting on Israel's true throne.

Unfortunately, for the great majority of the Israelites, their God had become nothing more than a ritual. They had forgotten His dealings and His blessings and had given themselves over to the worship of other gods. For them, Jehovah had become just another god.

Ahab was the king and had joined himself to a foreign

wife and opened the gates for idolatry to flood Israel. Baal worship, a "politically correct" sect, had become the religion of choice. The children of Israel had allowed themselves to be enticed by it, and the result was apostasy. They now considered Jehovah as old-fashioned or "politically unacceptable."

Elijah stood firm. He was not driven by society's whims and knew that Jehovah was the only true God. The old prophet fixed his eyes and tuned his ears, not yielding his heart to any other god. His unwavering conviction allowed him to boldly enter Ahab's courts and declare: *"As the LORD God of Israel liveth ..."*

Our world considers God to be old-fashioned and points people to the New Age, a "politically correct" religion whose prominent figure is Mother Earth. Men are taught today that they themselves are gods and that each individual has all the energy necessary to produce life, to heal themselves, and to perform miracles.

Everywhere you look, psychics are predicting someone's future or leading them through some sort of inner-healing. The New Age movement is telling everyone that they should worship in any way that makes them feel comfortable. They say that "god" is a generic term covering all deity, in symbol, or in figure. New Agers promote "out of body" experiences as the way to handle life's problems. They say that if it *feels* right, it must *be* right. Even in some supposedly Christian circles, Mother-Earth worship has replaced the worship of Father God.

This must stop! The Christian Church must be truly convinced that God is alive and that He is sitting upon His throne. As the church at large faces swaying beliefs and compromise, the Lord's true people must hold fast to the precepts of His Word.

Jesus didn't alter, bend, or compromise any portion of

God's law when He walked this Earth. He taught and demonstrated with His own life how to live, upholding a righteous standard in the midst of idolatry, lawlessness, and wickedness.

I believe that the world is looking to the Church for such a standard. Unfortunately, the devil has deceitfully charmed many Christians into believing that if they lower their standards, demanding less holiness, they can win more souls for Christ and build larger congregations. However, there isn't a single example in the life or ministry of Christ in which He watered-down, dressed-up, or softened the Kingdom message. Jesus didn't become a sinner so that He could better relate to sinners. He didn't become a harlot so that He could understand fornication. With judgment and mercy He told the adulteress, *"Go, and sin no more."*

In many of churches today, the existing priesthood exudes flesh, like Eli did. But the time has come for the flesh to die. God's Zadoks will walk uprightly before Him. And, like Elijah, they will stand boldly in heathen courts and declare, *"As the LORD God of Israel liveth ... ."*

Elijah's boldness wasn't the product of merely knowing about God. People everywhere know something about God, and they often have a form of godliness. Some go so far as to pray to Him. They may even read about Him or listen to Christian programs on radio and television. In some cases, these people even attend church. But head knowledge isn't enough.

Many Christians are caught up with God knowledge. There are Bible schools, libraries, computer programs, conferences, workshops, and much more, all designed to fit many needs and aspects of faith. I'm not against any of these. They can be a vital part of passing on faith from one generation to the next. There is a problem, however, when we solely pass on information, instead of revelation, and technology becomes a shortcut in an attempt to replace study and prayer. I cannot favor such efforts.

Knowledge, simply for the sake of knowledge, is empty. When Christians become aware that their knowledge is only as deep as their relationship with God, then they will become rich. There are very capable individuals who know a great deal. They may be able to quote many Scriptures and lock into theological debates, but when I look at their lives, I fail to see a depth of relationship that should accompany such knowledge.

Elijah's strength was his living and breathing relationship with God. On the day that he went before King Ahab, he was not afraid, knowing that he was standing in the presence of Almighty God. Was Elijah blind? Could he not see that he was standing in front of King Ahab? Should he not have feared King Ahab's power? Could not the king serve him life or death? To Elijah, his physical circumstances were secondary. He knew where he really stood — before the King of kings.

Elijah lived in the reality of his God, therefore he didn't fear King Ahab's wrath. He did fear disobeying his Lord. God was more of a reality to him than the flesh and blood that stood before his eyes. He lived in the conviction that his habitation and residence were with God.

What declaration do our lives make to others? Is it apparent to them where we find our dwelling? Do we live in the reality that He is our living God? Do we walk in the fear of man more than in the fear of the Lord? Do we walk with Him daily or just an hour on Sunday?

I believe that we are living the day that Isaiah proclaimed. Darkness fills the Earth. Gross darkness fills people's hearts and minds. Every day and every moment the media declares moral decay and violence. It's running rampantly throughout the world.

Elijah faced the darkness of his time with the knowledge and the revelation that comes from a face-to-face relationship with God. Because of this, he fearlessly decreed the Lord's judgment.

I have many acquaintances, but not all of them are equally well known. Some of them I simply greet at my front door. Our relationship is based on necessity: the mailman, the paper boy, a salesman, a florist. Others can come past my front door and enter the formal living room. There we can talk about the weather, current affairs, and even some spiritual things. There is a small group, however, that I bring past the front door, past the living room and into my kitchen. There we sit together and break bread in sweet communion around the table. We talk about our daily lives and lift each other up in prayer, sharing our testimonies and our burdens.

These individuals know me on a first-name basis. They know what kind of food I like. They know my favorite color and some of my other likes and dislikes as well.

There are some friends who are even more intimate. We bring them into our family room, just like any other part of the family. They are welcome to leisurely recline and take their shoes off if they want. We play games together, laugh and cry. We share our faults, our failures, and our accomplishments. We know each other in a very personal way.

Then there is my bedroom, and only one person, my husband, is welcome there. In the bedroom my husband and I are lovers. He knows me in a way that no one else does. My husband and I have a relationship in that room that is different from the relationship we have in the family room. In the family room, there are many distractions:

the children are romping about looking for attention, the television may be on, and many other things are going on. When we enter the bedroom, however, we leave distractions outside. We don't discuss our finances, the job, the ministry, or the children (at least we try to avoid those subjects). The bedroom is ours alone, and because we have spent time, face to face, undistracted in communication, we have true relationship. The light of intimacy changes our knowledge of each other from the factual to the relational.

When I became Mrs. Patrick Duggan, I received all the rights, the authority and the benefits that title brought to me. It was only as I spent face-to-face time with my husband, however, that I begin to understand what that meant. I had some knowledge of my rights and benefits, but my understanding of his heart, mind, will, and emotions took time to develop. Now, because I have spent time with him, I can carry out his desires, using the rights and the authority he has given me. I have a revelation of his heart. If faced with a situation in his absence, I pretty well know how he would handle it. With my delegated authority, I can carry out his will, according to his desires.

Elijah knew God's Word and God's desires because he had spent time with His Master in worship. Because of this, he could boldly stand and say, *"There shall not be dew nor rain these years, but according to my word."*

Elijah knew his God. He knew His statues and His ordinances. He knew that he could declare God's judgment and all of Heaven would back him up. Too often people walk and talk presumptuously. They claim things amiss and know nothing about God's will or heart concerning the matter. They haven't spent face-to-face time with Him, and they don't know His will.

Seekers of His Face

But Elijah did! He knew that God had spoken through his servant Moses concerning other gods and idolatry (see Deuteronomy 11:16-19). Elijah knew the Word of the Lord. Therefore, he spoke with conviction, with boldness, and with confidence. Without intimate relational face-to-face knowledge of God, one cannot make bold declarations of His will.

Facing immorality, compromise, lawlessness, or idolatry, how do we react? Do we react as Christ would have? Or do we compromise and sweep it under the rug? Does a righteous indignation rise up within us, causing us to confront such behavior? Or do we shyly take the back seat and keep quiet? When facing prejudice, injustice, or heresy, we shouldn't have to guess about what to do, or how to react. If we've spent time in communion, face to face, and we know God's heart, have His wisdom, understand His judgments, and exercise His mercy, we will be ready to do His bidding. He has called His people to function in His attributes.

Elijah faithfully declared the Word of the Lord. God said it and Elijah spoke it forth — nothing more and nothing less.

And Elijah acted upon what he knew. He announced that there would be neither rain nor dew until he said so. Without regard for his own fate, he pronounced God's judgment (after all, he too was an inhabitant of the land and would suffer from the drought, just as others would).

Elijah had God's Word, and he sought no more. Many times God's servants want to know more. They want more prophetic words to confirm the first message. Elijah didn't need more. He had all he needed to know. He knew it wasn't going to rain — period. He walked in obedience and relationship and nothing else was necessary.

Believers often fail to walk in simple obedience to the

first word God gives them, expecting all the while to be blessed with yet another. Only after Elijah walked faithfully in what he knew did God add further instruction:

> *GET THEE HENCE, and turn thee eastward, and hide thyself by the brook Cherith, that is before Jordan. And it shall be, that thou shalt drink of the brook; and I have commanded the ravens to feed thee there.* 1 Kings 17:3-4

Elijah accepted the Lord's instruction and turned eastward. He came to rest on the edge of a brook. It looked as if Elijah had escaped and that he was home free. After all, God had delivered him in the past, but there was a problem. This place of provision, where God had just sent him, was a dwindling brook.

If we were in the same situation, having been sent to a drying brook for provision, what would we do? Then, if God told us that our food would come by airmail (via an unclean raven), how would we have reacted?

Picture Elijah, sitting by the brook, with his feet dangling in the water, watching the reeds, and then noticing that the water is getting lower and lower each day. Quite often, when we face the drying-brook experience, we do one of two things, either doubt God's Word or rebuke the situation, blaming it on the enemy. A drying brook tests everything one knows and believes. A drying brook will develop character and sanctify lives. Elijah knew that the brook was drying, but he also knew that God would be faithful to the Word that he had given.

Eventually the brook did dry up completely. And where do we find Elijah at that moment? He was still by the brook where God had told him to stay (see 1 Kings 17:5-8). It's often easy to leave the place of instruction, promise, and provision when a dilemma presents itself.

Saying that Elijah faced a dilemma would be an understatement. But it didn't matter how low the brook got, Elijah remained faithful to God's instructions.

I've often seen people leave a church that God had sent them to when things didn't work the way they wanted. When God sends you to a place, it won't always be what you expected, and it won't always be what you asked Him for, but it will be the place that He deems necessary for your walk with Him. You may be there to learn obedience or patience or some other attribute, but don't leave there until God has finished His work in you.

Elijah faithfully stuck it out, despite the circumstances (see 1 Kings 17:7-9), and when God was ready for him, He found the prophet exactly where He had left him. This is important. Often believers miss God's opportunity because they aren't where He wants them. They've run away before the right time.

Elijah received no new instructions from the Lord until the brook dried up. Then God directed him to go into the territory of the enemy. There he would find a widow without a penny to her name, who would take care of him.

The life of Elijah shows us clearly that God's ways are not our ways. He takes foolish things, weak things, and even unclean things, and ordains them as His instruments:

> *For ye see your calling, brethren, how that not many wise men after the flesh, not many mighty, not many noble, are called: BUT GOD HATH CHOSEN the foolish things of the world to confound the wise; and God hath chosen the weak things of the world to confound the things which are mighty; And base things of the world, and things which are despised, hath God chosen, yea, and things which are*

not, to bring to nought things that are: That no flesh should glory in his presence. 1 Corinthians 1:26-29

Elijah did just as the Lord instructed, without hesitation, and went to Zarephath (see 1 Kings 17:9-11). Upon entering the city, he saw a woman gathering sticks. He called her and asked her to get him some water. When she turned to do as he requested, he stopped her and asked her also for a morsel of bread. She replied:

As the LORD thy God liveth, I have not a cake, but an handful of meal in a barrel, and a little oil in a cruse: and, behold, I am gathering two sticks, that I may go in and dress it for me and my son, THAT WE MAY EAT IT, AND DIE. 1 Kings 17:12

If there had been a moment for Elijah to doubt God, this was it. What kind of God would send him to a poor widow who was preparing a last meal for her son and herself with the very last resources she had?

But Elijah didn't falter. He chose to speak to the situation:

And Elijah said unto her, FEAR NOT; go and do as thou hast said: but make me thereof a little cake first, and bring it unto me, and after make for thee and for thy son. For thus saith the LORD God of Israel, The barrel of meal shall not waste, neither shall the cruse of oil fail, until the day that the LORD sendeth rain upon the earth.

1 Kings 17:13-14

Again, Elijah showed that he knew the God in Whom he had believed. With great confidence, he spoke comfort, instruction, and blessing. This widow, who was preparing to die, needed to hear that word of comfort.

During these desperate times in which we live, the world needs a word of comfort from the Church. Everywhere one turns we see, hear, or read about crisis — about a world of hopeless individuals preparing to die.

Elijah spoke hope and peace into a severe situation, *"Fear not."* Those who know this peace, God's children, need to rise with confidence and tell anyone who is in despair, "Fear not." We have the same ability that Elijah had, and we have an even greater hope – Jesus. I truly believe that if the Church would walk in the reality of the living God, following and obeying Him precisely, we would speak life into the most devastating circumstances and see marvelous manifestations.

Soon after Elijah came to reside with the widow, her son suddenly fell sick and died (see 1 King 17:17-19). The woman asked Elijah, *"O thou man of God? art thou come unto me to call my sin to remembrance, and to slay my son?"* Evidently she conceived her son in an illicit act, and she thought the prophet had now brought judgment upon her.

Elijah told the woman to give him her son. She seems to have been slow in responding, so Elijah took her son from *"out of her bosom."* This is a picture of hidden sin. The woman's son, who was the fruit of sin, had become a part of her. He was not simply attached to her, or associated with her, but he had become a part of her. He was in her bosom, in her heart. It would take his death and the hand of the Lord, through Elijah, to remove the son, who represented her sin. Removal from her bosom illustrates that she held the sin close. She nurtured it and fed it. It had become a part of her, a familiar friend, although her sin likely haunted her in the night seasons.

Christ wants to take away from us all the hidden areas that we hold to and nurture, and remove their dead works from us. He wants to free us of past sins that haunt us. As the prophet stretched out His hand to the widow, so does Christ, seeking to remove sin from our bosom.

Often hidden sin has been so well nursed in our bosom that it is a part of who we are and to remove it would create an emptiness, or void. But when God removes something, He always fills the emptiness with something new. Whatever we choose to give to him, He takes it and breathes His life into it; and when He gives it back, death is made life, and what we gave Him is not what it was, but rather a new creation (see 2 Corinthians 5:17). And once God has freed us from the sin that we held so close to our bosom, we are able to minister life to others in the same situation.

Elijah took the boy and laid his corpse on his bed. Then, the Scriptures tell us, Elijah cried unto God for the boy's life (see King 17:20-24). The Lord, hearing Elijah's cry, returned the boy's breath to his body. Elijah then carried the boy down the stairs and placed him in his mother's arms. The boy, who was once a reminder of sin and pain, was now a reminder of God's Word and promise.

Elijah was a man who lived in the knowledge of His Lord. He was a man who had a personal relationship with the Savior. He didn't seek the Lord for what he thought he could get out of Him, but rather for relationship. And because of this Elijah knew that God hadn't dealt evil to the widow, and he could move with confidence in this case. Because of his relationship with God, he could boldly pronounce God's judgments and God's mercy.

Seekers of His hand can't see past what God holds in His hands or provides. They aren't content unless He is doing something in or for them. They do not praise Him unless He provides. They try to keep Him within the arena of acts and works. They look to manifestations and experiences as a barometer that shows His presence.

Elijah was a seeker of God's face. He bowed before Him simply because of Who He was, not because of anything He could do for the prophet. He worshiped God simply because He was worthy to be worshiped.

When any believer knows God, he or she can declare life to those in hopeless situations, speak peace in turmoil, and share joy in mourning. Life will then come out of death.

What will be your choice? Will you seek His hand? Or will you be among the *Seekers of His Face*?

PART IV:

THE WORSHIP OF TWO COMPANIES

CHAPTER FIFTEEN

THE SOUNDS OF THE SANCTUARY

*A nd they sing the song of Moses the servant of God,
AND THE SONG OF THE LAMB, saying,
Great and marvellous are thy works, Lord God
Almighty; just and true are thy ways, thou King of saints.
Who shall not fear thee, O Lord, and glorify thy name? for
thou only art holy: for all nations shall come and worship
before thee; for thy judgments are made manifest.*

Revelation 15:3-4

There is a twofold revelation being birthed in the
Church: the revelation of communion and the revelation
of union. Everywhere I turn I hear of churches that are
feeling an urgency to come together with one purpose,
and that one purpose is to worship God.

Recently I have found myself teaching about the Bride,
everything from her preparation and attire, to her walk.
One day, while I was in worship, something happened
and I heard God's voice speak clearly and simply, in one
sentence, a summation of everything I had been teaching, "The preparation of the Bride is the revelation of the
Bridegroom." This revelation and its reality changed my
understanding of the Bride and my approach to sharing

this message. The word "revelation" means *a disclosure, or manifestation*, by God to man, of Himself and His will.

When Patrick and I were dating, we went through many phases. Our relationship grew and developed as we spent time together. Soon the topic of marriage began creeping into our conversations, and we concluded that matrimony was in our future.

Even though I had the knowledge that I would one day become a bride, I didn't have the revelation. It was my hope, but not a reality. That reality didn't come until the night Patrick took my hand, asked me to be his wife and placed the ring upon my finger. It was then that I had the revelation of my bridegroom. From that moment on, I no longer saw him as my boyfriend, but as my fiancé, my bridegroom. And when I got this revelation, I immediately began making preparations for my wedding. Before that moment I only had a certain knowledge about becoming a bride, but the reality of a ring changed my vision.

Unless we walk in the revelation of God's promise, we walk only in its knowledge. In order for the knowledge of a promise to become a revelation, we must be able to hear, see, and receive. God seeks communion and fellowship with man. He still walks among His people, drawing them, and compelling them to come near to Him.

Several months ago I heard the Holy Spirit tell me, "Listen to the sounds of the sanctuary." I inclined my ear and began to hear mighty winds and many voices, exclaiming together, "Holy, Holy, Holy, Oh Ancient of Days, Worthy are You to receive glory and honor and praise."

I was reminded of something similar that John saw:

> *And they sing the song of Moses the servant of God, and the song of the Lamb, saying, Great and marvellous are*

The Sounds of the Sanctuary

*thy works, Lord God Almighty; just and true are thy ways,
thou King of saints. Who shall not fear thee, O Lord, and
glorify thy name? for thou only art holy: for all nations
shall come and worship before thee; for thy judgments are
made manifest.*   Revelation 15:3-4

There is a song lifted up before the throne, and that
song declares the mighty deeds and the holiness of the
Lamb. In this song there is a call to the heart of man, a
call that seeks a response:

*DEEP CALLETH UNTO DEEP at the noise of thy water-
spouts: all thy waves and thy billows are gone over me.*
                                                   Psalm 42:7

God's call to communion and union have their origin
in His heart and emanate from His throne.

A fresh sound is going forth across the land. It is a song
that declares, "Holy, Holy, Holy." The words to the song
aren't, "Omnipresent, Omnipresent, Omnipresent." Neither is the score, "Glory, Glory, Glory." Of course both of
these alternatives would be true, and they are wonderful, but the chosen score proclaims, "Holy, Holy, Holy."
Seeing God in all of His splendor brings a cry that lifts
from deep within our spirits, "Holy, Holy, Holy."

Everything He is, and everything He does, is encom-
passed in His holiness. Man, from the beginning, has been
faced with God's holiness and has attempted to escape it
but always fails. God's holiness cannot tolerate sin, and
God's holiness moved Him to implement the plan of redemption. Man cannot approach God's throne without
holiness.

I truly believe that a fresh wind of holiness is sweep-
ing this land. God is calling for holy lives and holy

worship. We have tried to approach God based on fleshly righteousness for too long (see Micah 2:13).

God seeks a place to abide within each believer (see 1 Corinthians 6:19-20). He cannot dwell within unholy temples. His people must be set apart and consecrated unto Him as a holy habitation.

In these final chapters our attention will focus on the Tabernacle of Moses as a type and shadow of the spiritual tabernacle that is resident within each believer. God, in days of old, resided among His people in a specific place. In Moses's time, it was in the Tabernacle. In David's time, it was in a tent. In Solomon's time, it was in the Temple. Today, God has chosen not to live in a house made of stone, but in men's hearts.

In the Tabernacle of Moses there is much that teaches fellowship, communion and worship. As believers, we approach and commune with God in much the same way as the Levites. God said:

> *My eyes shall be upon the faithful of the land, that they may dwell with me; He who walks in a blameless way is the one who will minister to me.* Psalm 101:6 (NAS)

The Tabernacle of Moses found its origin in the heart of God. He designed it as His own dwelling place among the children of Israel. It was a place of ministry and worship.

God's instructions to Moses were specific and concerned every detail for construction and placement of the Tabernacle (see Exodus 25:8-9). It was arranged and fashioned according to God's pattern.

There is a thread that runs throughout the Tabernacle design: redemption and the cross. The Tabernacle sat in the midst of the camp, just as Christ dwells in the midst

The Sounds of the Sanctuary

of His people (see Matthew 18:20). In Israel there were twelve tribes divided into four groups. On the East side were the tribes of Judah, Issachar, and Zebulun (see Numbers 2:3-9). They totaled 186,000 and made up the largest of the four groups. On the South side were Reuben, Simeon, and Gad (see Numbers 2:10-16). This camp comprised 151,450 Israelites. On the West side, were three tribes: Ephraim, Manasseh, and Benjamin (see Numbers 2:18-24). This was the smallest group, with only 108,000 Israelites. On the North side were the three tribes, Dan, Asher, and Naphtali. This camp had 157,000 souls (see Numbers 2:25-31).

With the Tabernacle positioned at the point of intersection of the camps, the tribes around it formed the shape of a cross (if viewed from above). Not only did God give specific instructions concerning the placement of the Tabernacle, but He also gave specific instructions concerning its furniture, materials, courts, and who would maintain it. Each detail showed, in figure, the story of salvation, redemption, and relationship, and no detail was insignificant. The message God was showing through the Tabernacle pointed to Christ's finished work at Calvary.

The book of Hebrews reveals that the Tabernacle of Moses is a figure of the Heavenly Tabernacle:

Now of the things which we have spoken this is the sum: We have such an high priest, who is set on the right hand of the throne of the Majesty in the heavens; A minister of the sanctuary, and OF THE TRUE TABERNACLE, which the Lord pitched, and not man. For every high priest is ordained to offer gifts and sacrifices: wherefore it is of necessity that this man have somewhat also to offer. For if he were on earth, he should not be a priest, seeing that there are priests that offer gifts according to the law: Who serve unto THE EXAMPLE AND SHADOW OF HEAVENLY THINGS, as Moses was admonished of God when he was about to make the tabernacle: for, See, saith he, that thou make all things according to the pattern shewed to thee in the mount. But now hath he obtained a more excellent ministry, by how much also he is the mediator of a better covenant, which was established upon better promises.

Hebrews 8:1-6

All the contents of the Tabernacle, designed after a masterful pattern, bring us understanding in the work of a sovereign God. As we enter into the heavenly sanctuary and observe, listen attentively, for every detail cries out, "Holy, Holy, Holy." Entering into His holiness, God's people will find the communion and union that the Tabernacle foreshadows.

CHAPTER SIXTEEN

THE OUTER COURT:
THE LAMB UPON THE ALTAR

*A*nd thou shalt make the court of the tabernacle: for the south side southward there shall be hangings for the court of fine twined linen OF AN HUNDRED CUBITS LONG FOR ONE SIDE: And the twenty pillars thereof and their twenty sockets shall be of brass; the hooks of the pillars and their fillets shall be of silver. And likewise for the north side in length there shall be hangings of an hundred cubits long, and his twenty pillars and their twenty sockets of brass; the hooks of the pillars and their fillets of silver. And for the breadth of the court on the west side shall be hangings of fifty cubits: their pillars ten, and their sockets ten. And the breadth of the court on the east side EASTWARD SHALL BE FIFTY CUBITS. The hangings of one side of the gate shall be fifteen cubits: their pillars three, and their sockets three.

Exodus 27:9-14

When approaching the Tabernacle of Moses, the first thing one would have seen were curtains hanging around the outer court. This court was a perfect rectangle, one hundred cubits in length and fifty cubits in breath. Fine linen curtains, held by pillars, sockets, cords, and pegs, hedged the court.

The fine linen curtains that acted as a separation had a twofold function. First, they divided the outside from the inside. Secondly, they kept out those who were not serious in their approach to God's dwelling.

Once an individual was within this court, surrounded by the curtains, they were shielded, or protected, from the outside. God longed for His people to enter and find rest (see Psalm 84:2-10). David taught us how to enter:

> *Enter into his gates with thanksgiving, and into HIS COURTS WITH PRAISE: be thankful unto him, and bless his name.* Psalm 100:4

We are to enter His courts with praise, for it is a place of rejoicing. There they found forgiveness from their sins and sanctification for their walk.

This court had only one entrance. Therefore, there was only one way in, and one way out. The court was available to everyone, leader and layman, alike, and both had to enter by the same door. There was no side entrance or back entrance. Everyone had to enter the same way. This speaks to us of Jesus, for He is THE WAY and the only way (see John 14:6). He alone is the Door and all must enter through Him. There are no exceptions. There are no big shots before the altar of sin. All come the same way, through the same door, and to the same court.

In order to gain entrance to this court, one had to pull back a curtain. It had to be a deliberate act. No one entered by accident: stumbling in, backing in, falling in, or sliding in. Each individual had the responsibility of entering of their own will and by their own power.

Upon entering the court the children of Israel found two pieces of furniture: the brazen altar and the brazen laver. The altar was the only piece of furniture that had direct application to the congregation of Israel. In execution of their ministry, the priests used all the other pieces of furniture.

The brazen altar was the place of sacrifice. The word "altar" means *lifted up* or *ascended place*. It also means *the place of slaughter*. The innocent lamb upon the ascended place is an image of the innocent Lamb, Jesus, upon the altar. Calvary's tree was the place where men slaughtered the perfect Lamb. In crucifixion, He spilled His blood for sin; in resurrection, He placed His blood upon Heaven's Mercy Seat. He ascended and now sits as our Great High Priest (see Hebrews 3:1).

Of the Tabernacle altar, the Scriptures say:

> *And thou shalt make an altar of shittim wood, five cubits long, and five cubits broad; the altar shall be foursquare: and the height thereof shall be three cubits.*
>
> Exodus 27:1-3

At the brazen altar, which God commanded to be made of shittim wood (a durable knotty hardwood) and covered with brass, the priests carried out their duties, making atonement for the people. Brass, in Scripture, many times represents judgment.

> *And thou shalt make his pans to receive his ashes, and his shovels, and his basons, and his fleshhooks, and his firepans: all the vessels thereof thou shalt make of brass.*
>
> Exodus 27:3

These "pans" were used to carry the ashes from the fire of sacrifice outside the camp (Leviticus 6:10-11). "Fleshhooks" made it possible to arrange the sacrifices that were on the altar so that they would be consumed by the fire. "Firepans" and censers were used to carry the coals from the altar of sacrifice to the golden altar.

Upon the brazen altar, the priests made five offerings: the meat offering – sometimes called the meal or cereal offering (see Leviticus 2:1), the sin offering (see Leviticus 4:5-13), the peace offering – of which there were three kinds: wave offering, thank offering and heave offering – (see Leviticus 4:10), the sin offering – sometimes called the guilt offering – (see Leviticus 4:5-13), and the trespass offering (see Leviticus 5:15).

The first seven chapter of Leviticus present these five offerings and their fundamental message, the atoning of Calvary's altar (the cross). Before Jesus' death on the tree, there was no other place to make atonement for sins. It was the duty of the high priest to come before the people and make atonement for their sins. And Jesus is our High Priest:

> *Seeing then that we have A GREAT HIGH PRIEST, that is passed into the heavens, Jesus the Son of God, let us hold fast our profession.*   Hebrews 4:14

How privileged we are to have Jesus interceding for us! He has made atonement for our sins, once and forever.

Those that entered the outer court of the Tabernacle knelt before the altar of God. And once a year the high priest entered the Holy of Holies on the people's behalf.

Today, we bow before Jesus, the Lamb upon the altar, and enter at will. We can then lay our sins upon the altar of His sacrifice, the cross. If Jesus hadn't gone to Calvary, after entering the court, we would have bowed to an empty altar and further entrance would have been impossible. Because of the Lamb upon the altar, we may come boldly, anytime we're ready, and partake of the slain Lamb (see Hebrews 4:15-16). There is power in the blood of the Lamb, and in the word of our testimony (see Revelation 12:11).

When we come and wash in His blood, we are forever cleansed and forgiven of that sin that we have brought to His altar. If the Body of Christ would grasp this truth we would no longer walk as defeated servants, but rather as a redeemed army.

In the Kingdom of God there are no "exers:" no ex-drug addicts, no ex-alcoholics, and no ex-abusers. When any man or woman is washed in the blood of the Lamb, redemption becomes a reality. If you are washed in the blood of the Lamb, you are a new creature, a new creation. All those old things are passed away and forgotten.

"The word of their testimony" means victorious words, not the rehearsal of past sins. Believers must boldly declare that by the blood of the Lamb they have obtained victory, and they have been washed and purged.

Grasping the truth of what Jesus did will keep us triumphant, even when the enemy comes to taunt our minds with memories of the past. When a person has this understanding, he or she can stand in all confidence on the altar and tell the devil that the person he is talking about no longer exists.

Joel declared:

> *Let the priests, the ministers of the LORD, WEEP BE-TWEEN THE PORCH AND THE ALTAR, and let them say, Spare thy people, O LORD, and give not thine heritage to reproach, that the heathen should rule over them: wherefore should they say among the people, Where is their God?*
>
> Joel 2:17

In the outer court, before the Lamb's altar, God calls us to weep for those who would come after us to partake of His sacrifice, ministering as priests, praying, and interceding for the salvation of many. Many stand lost between the porch (the place of entrance) and the altar (the place of forgiveness). The Father's heart longs for all to be saved and that not one be lost. His desire is for all to come and to know the fullness of His abiding.

Another characteristic of the outer court of the Tabernacle was its noise. There were sounds from the people and sounds from the animals.

Several years ago, my parents (who are also pastors) and another pastor had the opportunity of going to Nigeria. While they were there, they were given the honor of dedicating the host pastor's son. The boy's parents had been trying to have a male child for many years, but had brought five daughters into the world.

Upon the birth of their son, the couple vowed that they would bring offerings of the best they had before the Lord to show their gratitude. Two of the offerings were a live goat and a live chicken. They tied the two animals in a side room, and during my father's message everyone could hear the goat and the chicken doing what was natural: clucking and naying. Then the chicken escaped, and my father soon found a clucking, pecking, chicken at his feet. That reminds me of what the outer court must have been like. There were many distractions in that place.

Not all the sounds were from animals. There was great weeping and great celebration in the outer court. In my own experience, there have been times when I approached the altar of God sorrowfully, under deep conviction, weeping in shame and sorrow because of my sin. But when I had touched the throne of grace, my sorrow turned to joy, for I knew that my shame was borne upon Calvary's cross and that I didn't have to carry the burden of guilt any longer.

On the cross, Jesus bore not only the filth of sin, but He also took upon Himself its guilt, shame, and burden. When we give Him our sin, He also takes its weight and its power from us. So when I come to the altar of grace I can lay at His feet my sin and my burden, and then walk away rejoicing in His mercy and grace.

There was no roof over the outer court, and the sun's intense light shone upon those who were there. This is symbolic of mixture. It is in the Outer Court that we leave the mixture behind. It was a place lit by natural means. But God had a different way, the glory light of the Holiest of All, but first we had to put to death all that would weigh us down. God wisely allows us to pass by the altar first, for there we can crucify and put to death all of our sins.

> *And the LORD spake unto Moses, saying, Thou shalt also make a laver of brass, and his foot also of brass, TO WASH WITHAL: and thou shalt put it between the tabernacle of the congregation and the altar, and thou shalt put water therein. For Aaron and his sons shall wash their hands and their feet thereat: When they go into the tabernacle of the congregation, they shall wash with water, that they die not; or when they come near to the altar to minister, to burn offering made by fire unto the LORD:* Exodus 30:17-20

When the priests entered, they first went to the altar to partake of the slain lamb. Next they passed on to the laver and washed. God provided the brazen laver so that all the effects of sin could be washed away.

Another reason for washing in the brazen laver was that the priest had to change his garments and leave all defilement in the cleansing waters before entering the Holy Place. When he had washed his hands and changed his garments he was ready to venture in and minister before the Lord.

Mirrors which the children of Israel had brought out of Egypt were used in making the laver (see Exodus 38:8). Just as the sacrifice was placed upon an altar of brass and all areas of sin judged, so also, the laver of brass, with its mirrors, judged the priests in all of their areas of service. As the priests washed in the waters of the laver, the mirrors reflected, constantly reminding, and exposing every area of the priest's life. The priests could thus see their need for cleansing, just like the people they ministered to. The mirrors not only helped remind them of their need for sanctification, but they also reminded them that they were a reflection, or representation, of God before His people.

Ministers must never lose sight of their responsibility to the people God has given them. They must know that they are reflections and representatives of God. Those that would minister before men also minister to God and before God. If ministers will walk in this noble understanding, God's people will pleasure in the purity of ministry and see a reflection of His attributes.

I believe that if more ministers would keep a correct perspective concerning ministry, we would see fewer individuals hurt in churches. How sorrowful it is to see sheep whose shepherd has kicked them!

Throughout Scripture Christ is compared to a shepherd (see Hebrews 13:20). There are many valuable traits in a shepherd, which are important in ministry. Pastors and ministers would do well to pattern themselves after such natural traits. Jesus is the Great Shepherd, and He is our example. He calls us to reflect His traits.

The Outer Court: The Lamb Upon the Altar

As a young child I experienced love, kindness, and tenderness from a wonderful father. He was always there. He educated, protected, disciplined, and nurtured me. He even played with me. So when I heard that God was my heavenly Father, it was easy for me to accept His love, forgiveness, correction, and instruction.

Ministers can give an impression, or present a reflection, that will either help or hinder God's move and work in the lives of those with whom we come in contact. Improperly handled sheep, those which have been cast aside or neglected, whether it be for lack of time, or because the shepherd wouldn't make time for them, will carry lasting impressions and ugly scars. Sheep that are bruised, battered, neglected, shunned, or improperly sheared – which can cause serious infections — will not easily follow their shepherd.

A shepherd comes into his job knowing that it is hard, frustrating, and thankless. Therefore, he or she shouldn't be surprised when the job turns out to be everything it was expected to be. Protection and nurture of sheep are the principal jobs of the shepherd.

A shepherd should know that sheep can and do bite, but a good shepherd won't raise their his to improperly harm his sheep. Rather, the shepherd must move in wisdom and grace to fend off the approaching snarl.

Effective shepherds know how to use their tools. When a stranger, or wolf, is among the sheep, he or she should use a staff, or look in the shepherd's bag, as did David, when facing the Philistine:

> *And he took HIS STAFF in his hand, and chose him five smooth stones out of the brook, and put them in A SHEPHERD'S BAG which he had, even in a scrip; and his sling was in his hand: and he drew near to the Philistine.*
>
> 1 Samuel 17:40

A shepherd's bag might include sticks, stones, or perhaps a knife fashioned from an old antler or claw.

A shepherd has duties: to spot impending danger and to find greens with the proper balance of nutrients to nourish the flock. He or she also looks at the condition of each individual sheep. If there is one that keeps going astray, the shepherd may lovingly break its leg with his staff. The shepherd does not abandon such a sheep, but carefully lifts it, carrying it on sturdy shoulders, where the sheep remains until its leg has mended. When it is well enough to walk on its own, it will be lowered to the ground by the shepherd's side, where it will always be found from then on.

We must look into God's glass:

> But we all, with open face BEHOLDING AS IN A GLASS the glory of the Lord, are changed into the same image from glory to glory, even as by the Spirit of the Lord.
>
> 2 Corinthians 3:18

Those that would be ministering priests, shepherds of God's people, will find that the way of preparation takes them to the brazen laver where they must wash and be reminded of God's call to service. *"To wash withal"* are words that summarize the primary function of the laver (Exodus 30:18). The old saying is, "Cleanliness is next to godliness." Although the Pharisees committed the error of believing that by keeping their hands clean they could get to Heaven, God would have a pure, holy, and clean priesthood.

In the outer court there were two substances for cleansing: water and blood. The Bible emphasizes these two elements. Water and blood provide rich shadows of Jesus' work of redemption on the cross (see John 19:34). When

The Outer Court: The Lamb Upon the Altar

Jesus' side was pierced, *"blood and water"* poured out for the cleansing of all who would believe. Jesus then provided, by His own sacrifice, everything that is needed to cleanse the worst sinner.

In the outer court we come to praise Him for what He has done in our lives. This is thanksgiving. He has saved us, delivered us, and washed us (see Psalm 116:19).

In the outer court we minister to one another, lifting up one another's burdens, strengthening ourselves in God to overcome our shortcomings, and before a holy altar we stand, washing one another with the water of His Word.

Now, we are ready to move a bit deeper into the Tabernacle, to enter the Holy Place and focus on the Lamb upon the Table.

CHAPTER SEVENTEEN

THE HOLY PLACE:
THE LAMB UPON THE TABLE

*T*hen *Jesus said unto them, Verily, verily, I
say unto you, Moses gave you not that bread
from heaven; but my Father giveth you the true
bread from heaven. For the bread of God is he which cometh
down from heaven, and giveth life unto the world. Then
said they unto him, Lord, evermore give us this bread. And
Jesus said unto them, I AM THE BREAD OF LIFE: he
that cometh to me shall never hunger; and he that believeth
on me shall never thirst.* John 6:32-35

Before the priests (who represent New Testament believers) could enter the Holy Place, they had to wash in
the laver, change their garments, and partake of the altar
(which represents Christ). It was impossible to bypass or
neglect these steps. Christians who desire to find the
deeper things of God must first prepare themselves –
washing, changing their spiritual garments, and partaking of the Lamb upon the altar. Only then can they hope
to enter the Holy Place, the second chamber of the wilderness Tabernacle.

Within the Holy Place there are no longer any distrac-
tion and no mixture. Those truths learned in the outer

court provide a firm foundation (see Hebrews 6:1-3) and with that foundation now established, it is time to move on to greater things (see Hebrews 5:13-14).

In the Holy Place, there was no mixture because all mixture was to have been washed and burnt away in the Outer Court. Only the light of the golden candlestick, a singular source, was visible. The candlestick was made from pure gold and looked more like a lampstand than modern day candlesticks. It held oil and not wax. Wax candles burn, consuming themselves, but the lamp that occupied the Holy Place was sustained by a continual supply of oil. Morning and night the wick had to be trimmed so that it wouldn't become crusty from old oil.

From one main shaft, three branches proceeded on either side, forming the candlestick. This makes a beautiful picture of Jesus, the Vine (see John 15:5). In all, there were seven branches on the golden candlestick. Just as a vine's branches join to its shaft, believers find their place of abiding in *"the True Vine"* (John 15:1).

Burning day and night, the candlestick illuminated the Holy Place. Its oil came from pure olives – beaten and crushed. Jesus, also the fruit of the olive tree – symbol of the Jewish people (see Jeremiah 11:15) – was beaten and crushed. In His last hours at Gethsemane (which means *oil press*), He suffered the pressing and crushing that only the cross could bring. I believe that Christ was already carrying His cross long before they nailed Him to the tree (see Luke 9:23).

As Jesus prayed in the Garden, He was in such agony that He sweat drops of blood. His heartache over sin had begun in the Garden. When they placed the cross upon His shoulders, I believe its burden was light compared to the weight of sorrow that He bore. When they removed the cross from His shoulders, I'm certain that its weight still pressed upon His beaten body. Jesus' beating and pressing opened the way for each believer to experience the Anointed One: the Holy Spirit.

Day and night, the candlestick required maintenance by the high priest (see Leviticus 24:3-4). He was to trim the wick, taking the old, crusty, burnt part away, and then fill the lamp with fresh oil. Without proper maintenance, there would have been an overabundance of smoke.

This shadow teaches New Testament priests to trim their wicks daily and fill their lamps with fresh oil (the Holy Spirit). Proper illumination will come only from those priests who watchfully care for their duties (see Revelation 16:15). God's Word gives many specific warnings that we must watch and keep ourselves ready at all times.

Of the ten virgins, five were wise and five were foolish. Those who were wise, knowing that the bridegroom would arrive soon, made the necessary preparations, while those who were foolish went about business as usual, and didn't make any preparations. Then all of them *slumbered and slept.*

To understand this parable, a look at Eastern culture is helpful. When a virgin was to be wed, she was told that her bridegroom would be coming and that she should make herself ready. She didn't know the exact hour that he would arrive, so she would make any necessary preparations and wait patiently until the hour was at hand.

The betrothal ceremony was celebrated between the two fathers well before the consummation of the marriage, and there are many similarities between the betrothal ceremony and the Passover Seder of Remembrance. In the Passover there are four cups: the cup of sanctification, the cup of remembrance, the cup of redemption and the cup of praise.

The bride's father and the groom's father would meet

in the betrothal and begin by partaking of the first cup —
the cup of sanctification. With this, they remembered that
marriage was a holy commitment and an act ordained
by God.

Then they would begin sipping from the second cup–
— the cup of remembrance. The girl's father would
recount all of his daughter's beautiful attributes, her talents, and any special abilities she might have, trying to
build up the wedding price. When the father entered the
house, his daughter may have been worth only two chick-
ens in the eyes of the groom's father, but by the time the
proud father of the bride is finished declaring her beauty
and virtues, she could be worth ten camels. Jesus has paid
the highest price for His Bride, His own blood (see 1
Corinthians 6:20).

After settling the wedding price, the parents would call
in the young girl. They poured a third cup, and turned a
second glass upside down. If she accepted the terms of
the arrangement, she would turn the glass over and pour
wine from the full glass into hers. Then she and her beloved would drink from the cup of redemption.

Christ's Bride drinks freely from redemption's cup. In
doing so, the believer becomes a joint heir with Him, and
a holy union is entered into. Jesus does not force us into
relationship, but stretches out His cup, offering us choice
wine.

Having reached this point, the couple would enter into
a legal union. The groom then went to prepare the bridal
chamber, and the young bride remained at home with her
father. The last cup, the cup of rejoicing, was filled on the
groom's return, at the wedding feast.

With all of these elements in mind, the last supper before Jesus' death, becomes rich in type and in shadow.
While the disciples partook of the cups at the last supper,

The Holy Place: The Lamb Upon the Table

Jesus told them, *"I will not drink henceforth of this fruit of the vine, until that day when I drink it new with you in my Father's kingdom,"* (Matthew 26:29).

It was customary, after the betrothal ceremony, for the bride to remain at home, still a virgin, until her bridegroom returned. First, he had to go and prepare a place for her. Jesus said:

> *Let not your heart be troubled: ye believe in God, believe also in me. In my Father's house are many mansions: if it were not so, I would have told you. I GO TO PREPARE A PLACE FOR YOU. And if I go and prepare a place for you, I will come again, and receive you unto myself; that where I am, there ye may be also.* John 14:1-3

In preparation for the groom, the bride — waiting still at home — changed her garments and veiled herself so that only her eyes could be seen. That was enough, for the eyes are the mirror of the soul.

During the days of her wait, which could be many, the young bride would go about town dressed in her betrothal garments. Others, looking upon her, knew that she was promised to another. Her beloved trusted her, and he knew that she would keep herself pure for him until he returned for her. Still, she didn't know the day or the hour of his return and had no choice but to wait patiently. A believer, having drunk of redemption's cup, enters into a union with the Beloved. At that point, those that have partaken of the cup must change their garments from worldly rags to holy garments and then watch and wait for the Husband's coming.

When others see the redeemed about town, or in the work place, they should see them wearing the garments of one promised. They should know that they look upon a separate people, pledged to another.

A girl who had entered into such a pact, partaking of the cup, was not free to participate in many of the activities of the other girls. Her habits had to change, and she couldn't be found in the old gathering places. She had to keep herself pure, clean, and spotless (see Revelation 15:15 and 19:7).

No longer can Christ's Church walk about with foolish minds and weakness of the flesh. His Church must walk with determination. They must keep themselves free from the lusts and desires of the flesh. He is Master, and He has paid the price for His bride. She is no longer free, but betrothed. As her Beloved's, her so-called "rights" are no longer valid, unless they line up with His Word. She can no longer justify her actions or activities based on those views and interpretations offered by her old friends. She must know that He asks for nothing less than holiness.

It was customary for the bridegroom to come in the middle of the night and steal his bride away. He would then take her to the chamber and consummate their union. The seal of their union and of the covenant they had made, was a show of blood. Upon seeing the blood, the bridegroom declared, "She is mine." He then hung the sheet out for all to see. He presented her with a wedding garment and together they drank from the final cup — the cup of rejoicing.

Scripture tells us that at midnight, the darkest hour, a cry was made, *"Behold, the bridegroom cometh; go ye out to meet him,"* (Matthew 25:6). This cry came while *"they all slumbered and slept."* If all were asleep, who made the call? Could it be a contradiction?

Perhaps Solomon provides an explanation:

I sleep, BUT MY HEART WAKETH: it is the voice of my

The Holy Place: The Lamb Upon the Table

beloved that knocketh, saying, Open to me, my sister, my
love, my dove, my undefiled: for my head is filled with dew,
and my locks with the drops of the night.

Song of Solomon 5:2

When the Bride has made herself ready, it matters not at what time of day or night her Beloved chooses to come. She will be there, ready to announce His arrival and to bid others to come to the feast.

Of all the sleeping virgins, one was awake in her heart – the bride. She sounded the call.

Today, a call should resound throughout the land. God's Church should be announcing, "Prepare ye the way, for behold the Bridegroom cometh." The heart of God's Bride has been stirred. It doesn't matter if she is asleep or if she's awake, her heart stirs with anticipation.

When the call came, all the virgins who had been asleep rose and trimmed their lamps. The foolish virgins said to the wise, *"Give us of your oil; for our lamps are gone out"* (Matthew 25:8). There is an imperative that the Beloved is showing his Bride in this parable: Keep your lamps full of fresh oil and fresh communion. Yesterday's oil and yesterday's communion won't do. Rise afresh each new morning, trim your wicks and fill your lamps with fresh oil.

The foolish virgins tried to borrow some oil from the wise, but the wisdom of the wise showed them that they only had enough for themselves. It would seem that the Lord is showing His people to get enough oil (representative of the Holy Spirit) for their own need, and to get it before it's too late. While the foolish virgins went to buy more oil, the bridegroom came.

An interesting detail about the call is that it preceded his arrival. Today, as never before, the announcement of

191

His coming is going out, and the Church is being told to prepare. Yesterday's oil, yesterday's relationship, won't be enough. The model presented by the parable is clear: Believers can be wise, and prepared, or they can be foolish, though still "virgins," and be locked out of the marriage feast.

When the foolish virgins returned, they knocked and begged, "*Lord, Lord, open to us,*" but He answered, "*I know them not.*" Not all answer preparation's call. They sit back, trusting yesterday's relationship, thinking that everything is fine. But it's not. They have run out of fresh oil.

The Scriptures are clear. Only those who have kept their garments clean and walk in fresh communion and fellowship while seeking God's face will enter the feast. Everyone has been called, but only those who have kept their commitment will be honored as the Lamb's wife. "*His WIFE hath made herself ready*" (Revelation 19:7).

The word used here to describes the Bride is "*wife.*" Wife, in Western culture, is usually reserved to speak of the bride after the consummation of the marriage, but in the East, the bride became a wife after the betrothal and, at that point, she began her preparations – before the consummation of the union.

Once saved, the believers' relationship begins, and they enter the time of waiting for their Beloved to come and sweep them away. They must then keep themselves pure of all defilement until the day they are taken at the Bridegroom's coming. When He arrives, He will be looking to see if His Church has kept herself pure, and if she is wearing the seal of His covenant, the blood of the Lamb.

Another important piece of furniture found in the Holy Place was the Table of Shewbread. It was positioned directly opposite the Golden Candlestick, and held twelve loaves of bread, representing the twelve tribes of Israel.

The Holy Place: The Lamb Upon the Table

All the tribes were represented, symbolizing that all of them together formed one body. The priests ate the shewbread.

This bread represents for us Christ, who is *"the Bread of life"* (see Matthew 5:14-16). And it represents His Body. Although there are great differences between us, we make up one great Body. There is unity upon the Lord's table. And it is this Body of believers that provides for God's ministers.

The shewbread was made of fine flour. The grain was milled, ground, pressed, and sifted. In analogy, Pontius Pilate found no fault with Jesus (see Luke 23:4). He was perfect, and even further milling, grinding, pressing and sifting in the tribunals of His accusers revealed no just cause for His crucifixion. He was the perfect, innocent sacrifice.

As the Bread of Life, He is upon the Table, awaiting those that would partake of Him. In the Outer Court, the believer partook of the Lamb upon the altar, but within the Holy Place, the Lamb is upon the table. At the table, there is sweet fellowship and communion. Partaking of the slain Lamb upon the Table makes the New Testament priest a participant in Christ's suffering and in His divine nature.

Through the things that Jesus suffered, He learned obedience (see Hebrews 5:8). Partaking of the Lamb makes those who participate one with Him. His ways become their ways. His will becomes their will. His desires become their desire.

Those who partake of the slain Lamb willingly follow their Lord, their Shepherd. When it's time to be sheared, as His obedient sheep, they willingly give up their fleece. They willingly go to His altar. They willingly follow His example:

*He was oppressed, and he was afflicted, yet he opened not
his mouth: he is brought as a lamb to the slaughter, and
AS A SHEEP BEFORE HER SHEARERS IS DUMB, so
he openeth not his mouth.*   Isaiah 53:7

Life brings shearing and that may not be a pleasant
process. The circumstances and difficulties of life may
stretch and strip our flesh, which we esteem so precious.
In all of this, we must remember that Jesus stood before
the shearers without complaining, and if we have been
to His table, we can do it too.

Partaking of the Lamb upon the Table makes Him our
sustenance. We will never find the Bread of His refined
texture stale or dry. At His table there can be no empty
ritual. It can never become a mere custom, something to
do every night before we go to bed, or something we do
every morning over cereal, part of a routine. Believers
should approach His table with expectation, for that is
where He patiently awaits to reveal Himself to those who
would approach.

While the priest stood at the Table of Shewbread in the
light of the candlestick and partook of holy sustenance,
there was a sweet fragrance that rose from the Altar of
Incense, the last piece of furniture in the Holy Place. This
wasn't like the Outer Court, where there were odors from
ashes, smoke, flesh, and blood. The incense of the Holy
Place was very special:

*And the LORD said unto Moses, Take unto thee sweet
spices, stacte, and onycha, and galbanum; these SWEET
SPICES with pure frankincense: of EACH SHALL THERE
BE A LIKE WEIGHT: And thou shalt make it a perfume,
a confection after the art of the apothecary, tempered together, pure and holy: And thou shalt beat some of it very*

The Holy Place: The Lamb Upon the Table

small, and put of it before the testimony in the tabernacle
of the congregation, where I will meet with thee: it shall be
unto you most holy.   Exodus 30:34-36

Every spice that was used to make this incense had to
be pure and salted, and the same weight of each one used.
Burning the resulting incense in the Holy Place would
have made a rising plume of smoke.

Incense is often associated with prayer (see Psalm 141:2
and Revelation 5:8), but as sometimes happens, there is
more than one valuable application in the Scriptures. This
cloud of incense was a sacrifice that rose in the Lord's
presence:

> *By him therefore let us offer the SACRIFICE OF PRAISE*
> *TO GOD CONTINUALLY, that is, the fruit of our lips*
> *giving thanks to his name.*   Hebrews 13:15

Such a *"sacrifice of praise"* comes from true worship (see
Jeremiah 33:10-11). This means that sincere adoration is
similar to the rising sweet fragrance of perfectly made
incense. It could not contain any imperfection. Even the
fire that burned it had to be perfect. As we have seen,
"strange fire" would bring devastating results. The fire had
to come from the Brazen Altar that sat in the Outer Court
and burned perpetually, having been lit by God Himself
on the day that Moses and Aaron dedicated the Tabernacle (see Leviticus 9:23-24, 16:12-13 and 6:12-13). God's
fire, which can speak of the Holy Spirit's workings, burns
away fleshly living, keeping His ministering priests pure
as they stand before His holy Table in service.

Worship, offered up in sacrifice, isn't always sweet in
God's nostrils. Sometimes it contains mixture and pro-
duces a stench. When this is true, God quickly rejects it.

Sometimes, ritualistic or rigid styles of worship can be "strange" in God's nostrils. It depends on the heart of the person offering it, but such habit-bound worship is always suspect. It is false to think that just because one lifts their hands in worship that God is under an obligation to automatically accept their sacrifice. He has no such imperative! He looks quickly at the censer to see what it contains – bitterness or love, tradition or sincerity.

We remember that Cain, who presumed to offer his own form of worship, Aaron's sons, who offered "strange fire," and Korah, who sought a function and a place that didn't pertain to him, were all met with God's rejection and judgment.

As the priests stood in the Holy Place of service ministering before, and unto the Lord, their service was either pleasing or displeasing. Today's priest minister either a satisfying fragrance or an unpleasant odor.

I love to minister God's Word to hungry hearts. I am overwhelmed each time I see an individual healed, delivered, or refreshed by the anointing of His Word. However, as a minister, I must stay keenly aware that my first responsibility is to God, serving and ministering unto Him as His priest. People may see me before them ministering, but my ministry began long before I stood behind that pulpit. I am under a moral and a spiritual obligation to approach ministry and service knowing that I'm first bound in service to God.

All Christian ministers and leaders must become keenly aware of what compounds are found in the incense they offer. Does the incense stink of an old perfume? Or does it have a fresh aroma, ready for God's altar? Have you brought stale bread? Or is it straight from the oven, ready for His table?

Several years ago I attended a conference where several leading ministers delivered eloquent messages from the Word of the Lord. One evening, as one of the speakers finished his message and walked off the platform, one of his assistants was waiting for him and flung a coat on his back and whisked him out the door. My heart was instantly grieved. It seemed that the ministry had only begun and was abruptly concluded.

I do not believe the Lord is happy with such orchestrations that have been forced upon the Body. I do understand the occasional need, but I believe it should be limited behavior and not the norm. I do not believe that God would have tolerated such behavior from his ministering priests, His hand outstretched.

By now it should be clear that every article of furniture in the Tabernacle was designed to point the way to God's promised redemption. Every task, every service, and every ministry pointed to Jesus.

The Levites, the priests, were no celebrities. They were simple men, known by their family and tribe. They had but one possession, and that was God. They were keenly aware of the fact that without Him they were nothing and had nothing.

God's ministers, today's priests, are not called by Him to be performers, mere actors. Men and women of God would do well to keep themselves rich in the simplicity of relationship with their Lord.

Servants of the Almighty should trim their wicks daily, ensuring that their flame burns clearly and without smoke. This takes fresh Holy Spirit oil; fresh communion with the Father. The product will be fresh bread and refined incense, free from mixture, to offer in the Holy Place.

In the Outer Court, God's people lifted up praise and thanksgiving for what He had **done** in their lives. There, His people were cleansed by blood and washed in the water of His Word.

Once inside the Holy Place, however, the service of the priests was not for man, but was performed unto a holy God. Entering the Holy Place, the priests laid aside their service to man. When the priests of today enter God's Holy Place, they should find their lips filled with thanksgiving and praise for what He **does** each day in their lives. He is the Bread upon the Table that sustains. He is the Light of the Candlestick. He is the Perfect Sacrifice of the Altar of Incense.

Having partaken of the Lamb upon the Table, and having been illuminated by His pure light and immersed in His sweet fragrance, we are prepared to enter into the Holiest of all. The Holy Place is wonderful, but it is now time to leave. Service to man, as performed in the Outer Court, and even service to God, as presented in the Holy Place, has its place. But now let us enter the Most Holy Place, where Christ, the center of our worship, dwells.

So lay aside for the moment all serving and ministering, and come into His presence, locking everything else outside, and let us fall before His throne and worship and adore Him as God.

CHAPTER EIGHTEEN

THE MOST HOLY PLACE: THE LAMB UPON THE THRONE

*W*hich hope we have as an anchor of the soul, both sure and stedfast, and which entereth into that within the veil; Whither THE FORERUNNER IS FOR US ENTERED, even Jesus, made an high priest for ever after the order of Melchisedec.

Hebrews 6:19-20

In the Outer Court the priests partook of the Lamb upon the Altar. In the Holy Place they partook of the Lamb upon the Table. But in the Most Holy Place, the high priest came face to face with the Ark of the Covenant, God's very presence, the Lamb upon the Throne.

Before the priests could enter the Most Holy Place they had to pass through the Veil. This veil was not a small curtain. It was made from *"blue, and purple, and scarlet, and fine twined linen of cunning work"* (Exodus 26:31). It was exceedingly thick, with multiple layers, and couldn't have been torn, or even cut, by common means.

This Veil sent a specific message: keep out. Once a year the high priest entered, no more. The Veil was a constant reminder of the separation that existed between God and man. It represented access to God's presence denied. But

Calvary changed all that, and God ripped the Veil in two (see Matthew 27:50-51). Now, because the Veil has been torn from top to bottom, believers may access the presence of God.

The Scriptures teach us the meaning of the Veil and the meaning of it being torn by the hand of God – although neither the wilderness Tabernacle, nor the Jerusalem Temple, with their veils, stands today. The Veil has been removed:

> *Let us therefore come boldly unto the throne of grace, that we may obtain mercy, and find grace to help in time of need.* Hebrews 4:16

> *Having therefore, brethren, BOLDNESS TO ENTER INTO THE HOLIEST BY THE BLOOD OF JESUS, By a new and living way, which he hath consecrated for us, THROUGH THE VEIL, that is to say, HIS FLESH; And having an high priest over the house of God; LET US DRAW NEAR with a true heart in full assurance of faith, having our hearts sprinkled from an evil conscience, and our bodies washed with pure water.* Hebrews 10:19-22

Before Christ came, men had no immediate access beyond the veil, but His death changed everything. As a consequence, the Veil provides a remarkable vista of Christ's life and death and of access to God's presence, once denied, made possible through redemption.

Those that have come under the blood of Jesus have free access and bold entrance into the very presence of God. It's now so easy to enter that many may do so flippantly, taking this privilege for granted. The phrase *"come boldly,"* however, doesn't mean to come presumptuously, hurriedly, or candidly.

The Most Holy Place: The Lamb Upon the Throne

When the veil was torn, God made access available to every believer, and all those who would could now enter into His presence without need of an intermediary. No longer was there any need to wait until the high priest carried in the blood on the Day of Atonement once a year. This is wonderful, but often misunderstood. The torn veil changed our access, but not our accountability.

"Come boldly" is what God calls His own to do every day. We may come before "the throne of grace" in our time of need, because there is no longer a need to wait for His forgiveness. Believers can enter into God's presence and fall upon His mercy and grace.

The blood of Jesus was the final sacrifice, and He has already presented it to the Father on our behalf, making us the recipients of His ultimate sacrifice, thus sealing the Old Covenant by His own blood. Yes, when we approach God's throne, His blood provides access, and His grace gives mercy (see Hebrews 7:26-27). But there is another aspect to this that we must consider. God's throne requires reverence and respect.

Even before the Veil was removed, the high priest did enter the Most Holy Place. In some way he passed beyond the barrier the Veil presented. Many have speculated about how the high priest may have accomplished this. Some have thought that God translated the high priest through the veil. This possibility brings the questions: What about responsibility? What accountability did the high priest have if his entrance was gained in this manner?

God gave specific instructions concerning every article of furniture in the Tabernacle, every garment, every sacrifice, and every ceremony. He made man responsible to carry out every detail and every instruction. Therefore, it seems likely that He would have required man to show responsibility when entering His holy presence. The high priest could not bypass nor neglect any step in his preparation to enter the Most Holy Place. Considering this, does translation make sense?

God demonstrated His character in every one of the Tabernacle's particulars. God wanted to establish a perfect pattern. Since God insisted upon instruction, responsibility, and accountability, I don't believe that He suddenly changed His ways when dealing with the high priest's entrance to perform ministry related duties in the presence of the Almighty.

Another school of thought proposes that the high priest slipped around the side of the veil. There is problem though. To slip around the side denotes a cunning maneuver, as if by scheming, entrance may be gained into the presence of God. And God doesn't operate deceitfully. Man's ways may be to hide, but God does things openly and aboveboard.

At the entrance of the Outer Court there was also a curtain. When people entered, they did it with a deliberate act, pulling back the entrance curtain. The Veil had no such entrance, for God didn't intend it to be a door, but a barrier. Even so, I believe that there was a proper way to enter the Most Holy Place.

A door is a barrier, unless it has some way to open it. Modern doors have keys. Was there a key to entering beyond the veil? God provided the master key to us by ripping the Veil open. Could it be that looking at the way God ripped open the Veil can point to the answer?

Everything God does has a purpose. He ripped open the Veil from top to bottom, not on one side or the other, not in a corner, and not even from side to side. That would imply that the priest, before God's action, entered at the same point that God opened it, but how?

The Most Holy Place: The Lamb Upon the Throne

In Scripture, God hasn't seen fit to give a precise revelation of the high priest's entrance, but a deeper look may be helpful. An important principle found throughout the Bible is that man cannot approach God by his own righteousness. When man encounters God's holy presence, the last thing of significance is self. Isaiah, when he beheld God's holiness, instantly saw the condition of his mortal body, and at once uttered:

> *Woe is me! for I am undone; because I am a man of unclean lips, and I dwell in the midst of a people of unclean lips: for mine eyes have seen the King, the LORD of hosts.*
> Isaiah 6:5

God required Moses to remove his shoes before approaching the burning bush. John, when he beheld the glory of the Lord, fell on his face, as though he were a dead man.

Throughout Scripture, whenever someone found themselves in God's holy presence, they responded by bowing, falling prostrate, or by declaring their unworthiness (see Isaiah 64:6).

Isaiah announced that man's righteousness is as *"filthy rags."* It's safe to assume that the high priest did not approach God by his own merits.

Considering all of these factors, and the awesome Ark of the Covenant itself, the very throne of God, I believe that the high priest must have approached God in much the same manner as Isaiah, Moses, and John. As the high priest approached the Most Holy Place, I believe that the very awareness of God's divine power, glory, and holiness, brought him to his knees. Thus he bowed, or prostrated himself, in a manner that allowed him to crawl under the Veil. In doing so, he would pass the Veil and everything the veil represented: separation from the world and covering by the blood of covenant (see Hebrews 10:19-22).

Christ's torn flesh separates His Bride from every other people. On Calvary His flesh was rent, and so too the Veil. For the high priest, the Veil was his covering as he entered the Most Holy Place.

Today believers enter the Most Holy Place, passing through the rent Veil, and must face their own personal Calvary, the place of God's dealing. There is only one way to approach the throne of grace, by way of Jesus' own sacrifice and God's dealing.

Some people seem to stay in the place of the rent Veil, not quite able to step through beyond God's dealings. Perhaps they think that by staying in the dealings of God they are in the presence of God. Yet they are merely standing in the door. Another step and they will find His presence.

Once inside the Most Holy Place the high priest came face to face with the Ark of Covenant, the Throne of God's presence. Everything else was now left behind. The only thing left was communion with God's glory, worshipping Him upon the Throne.

What God had done, or what He was doing, or even what He would do, was no longer an issue. It was the Most Holy Place, where the Lamb upon the Throne was proclaimed.

When the high priest passed under the Veil and into God's holy presence, he applied the blood of sacrifice and the throne of judgment became a throne of grace and mercy. The high priest could not enter without blood. Under the Old Covenant the blood of a bullock had to be applied once a year, but under the New Covenant Christ's blood has made the throne of judgment a throne of grace for all that would approach, covered by His blood.

The Most Holy Place: The Lamb Upon the Throne

Worship in the Most Holy Place is only possible by the blood, and for today's believer that means Christ's blood. Rejecting His blood is like removing the bloodstained Mercy Seat from the Ark (see 1 Samuel 6:19).

There can be no entrance apart from the blood of Christ. Without His blood, there is no Gospel, no good news.

It seems that many new contemporary songs, with their new sounds, neglect the blood of Christ. I don't know about you, but when I hear someone saying that "The Old Rugged Cross," "Amazing Grace," and "Oh, The Blood of Jesus," are old-fashioned, I think that person should quickly find an altar. Nothing could be more important than Jesus' precious blood.

In the Most Holy Place, service has been accomplished and distractions have been left outside. There is no mixture. There are only sounds of adoration from the heavenly sanctuary: *Blessing, and honour, and glory, and power, be unto him that sitteth upon the throne, and unto the Lamb for ever and ever"* (Revelation 5:13-14).

In the Outer Court we praise Him for what He has done. He is the Lamb upon the Altar. In the Holy Place we praise Him for what He does in our lives. He is the Lamb upon the Table. But in the Most Holy Place, we worship Him because He is our God, the Lamb upon the Throne.

Having seen that every part of the Tabernacle has an indelible meaning conveyed through types or shadows and that Jesus and His work shine forth through each of them, we are now called to make a choice: remain in the Outer Court, move into the Holy Place, or pass through the Veil and into the Most Holy Place. Many are content, seeking God's hand for continual deliverance in the Outer Court. Others will wash in His laver and let His redeeming power flow into them. Some make it to the Holy Place in the Inner Court. There they find the light of revelation and feast upon His table, enjoying the aroma of His incense. This is a wonderful place to be. Some say they feel goose bumps being here. But as wonderful as this place is, we must be willing to leave it behind and fall at His feet. Until we have pressed in and passed through the veil we will remain forever seekers of His hand.

Being a seeker of God's hand isn't all bad. It is even necessary, on a daily basis. We all need fresh bread from Heaven. There is a still deeper place awaiting us, however, beyond the veil – at the throne of God.

For those who would enter, not hurrying off ungratefully after receiving some favor from God's hand, beauty and fulfillment await. Before His throne, revelation becomes reality. Let us lay everything else aside and fall down before His throne.

WHERE WILL YOU ABIDE?

A *nd there shall in no wise enter into it any thing*
that defileth, neither whatsoever worketh abomin-
ation, or maketh a lie: BUT THEY WHICH ARE
WRITTEN IN THE LAMB'S BOOK OF LIFE.

Revelation 21:27

In conclusion, I would like to write a personal note, conveying what I believe is heavy upon God's heart. A call is going forth, emanating from the throne of God, drawing His people to come and abide closer to Him than ever before. He is standing at the door of each heart, knocking, trying to gain entrance. Some sit in a place of comfort and others bask in revelation's light. They can hardly be bothered to get up and open the door to Him. But He longs to stir His own and cause them to enter deeper than ever before.

God is calling us to look beyond position, race, and gender. Entrance into His throne room isn't determined by wealth or its lack, by gender or race. In the Church, segregation isn't part of God's plan, and Heaven certainly won't be divided by such distinctions. The Veil has been rent by Christ's work on Calvary, and petty notions must be left at the entrance of the Tabernacle.

AND HATH MADE OF ONE BLOOD ALL NATIONS
OF MEN for to dwell on all the face of the earth, and hath

determined the times before appointed, and the bounds of their habitation; That they should seek the Lord, if haply they might feel after him, and find him, though he be not far from every one of us: For in him we live, and move, and have our being; as certain also of your own poets have said, For WE ARE ALSO HIS OFFSPRING. Acts 17:26-28

God's people are one. There is one God, one Church, and one Bride. The ignorance and pride of humankind, their hatred and discord, may bring separation in this present age, but these considerations must vanish within His Church and will vanish when we pass beyond the Veil and bow at God's throne. There is only one division that God will make. He will divide the holy from the unholy, the righteous from the unrighteous.

God is calling His Body to be His Bride, and the wedding day is approaching. I am convinced that not all who have thought they were part of His Body will be present for the marriage. Some "virgins" will be foolishly looking for oil they should have been carrying.

Let us look past our private interpretations and positions, past our pet beliefs and revelations and let us see Jesus — the Lamb, our King, sitting on His throne. As Paul declared:

But we all, with open face beholding as in a glass the glory of the Lord, are changed into the same image from glory to glory, even as by the Spirit of the Lord.
2 Corinthians 3:18

It is my burden that none remain afar off, but that we all come to the place of worship before His holy throne.

Where Will You Abide?

Let us not be content with anything less than the presence of the Lamb.

Draw near. Know the sweetness of His lips, the breath of His nostrils, and the embrace of His eyes. He is altogether beautiful. Let us respond to His call and become *Seekers of His Face*.

Ministry address:

Cynthia Duggan
P.O. Box 1630
Mt. Pleasant, South Carolina 29465-1630
(803) 971-9001